I WONDER WHAT'S OUT THERE

A Vision of the Universe for Primary Classes

By
Joanne DeFilipp Alex
with
Aline D. Wolf

Parent Child Press Inc.
PO Box 675
Hollidaysburg PA 16648

Dedication

To island adventures off the coast of Maine and moon walks with my husband, Joe, our son Joel, and daughters Jessica and Julianna; our pets and the children I work with every day who all keep the sense of wonder alive for me.

Please Note

In some schools the word *Primary* refers to a class for three to six year-olds; in other schools a class for six to nine year-olds is called *Primary*. The Primary classroom described in this book is for three to six year-olds. However, many of the activities can also be used with children older than six.

Design: Jana Stanford Sidler

Page Layout: Diana M. Feathers

Photographs by Joanne DeFilipp Alex and the staff of Stillwater Montessori School

Library of Congress Control Number: #2002117643

ISBN # 0-939195-32-1

TABLE OF CONTENTS

"Let us give the child a vision of the whole universe…for all things are connected to form one whole unity." – Maria Montessori

"If a child is to keep his inborn sense of wonder…he needs the companionship of at least one adult who can share it, rediscovering with him the joy, excitement and mystery of the world we live in." – Rachel Carson

"In the end, we will preserve only what we love, we will love only what we understand, and we will understand only what we are taught." – Baba Dioum (conservationist from Senegal)

Introduction

Bringing some of the wonders of the universe to young children has been a project of Joanne Alex for the past several years. Each time I have visited her classroom for three through six year-olds, I have marveled at her creative ideas and urged her to share them with other professionals.

Joanne is a teacher who is gifted with remarkable insights into the nature and interests of children in their earliest years. She is also blessed with an exciting curiosity about space, a sense of wonder about the universe, and a profound respect for Planet Earth.

In 1998 Joanne Alex was chosen Teacher of the Year in the state of Maine. With this honor came the opportunity for her to attend International Space Camp in Huntsville, Alabama. With a group of teachers from many foreign countries, she was outfitted with a flight suit and participated in simulated space flights. This experience did not merely dazzle Joanne; it prompted her to reflect on how she could bring the wonders of space into her classroom. She asked herself, "How can I help children to realize that they are part of the universe?" "How can I help them to understand that Planet Earth is a very special place—the only planet in our solar system where life is possible?"

As a primary Montessori teacher, Joanne is well aware of the unique Cosmic Education Curriculum that is the heart of Montessori elementary classes[1]. In no way does her work pre-empt this elementary program, but it does whet the appetite of primary students for this later experience. The activities she describes here, however, are not only for children who are now, or eventually will be, in Montessori schools. They offer any child the excitement of taking his or her first steps into the wonders of the universe.

In a very real sense when children ask, "What's out there?" they are opening their minds and indicating their interest in learning not only about the moon, the sun and the stars, but also about the satellites and the space flights that they may have seen on television. Joanne uses Planet Earth and all familiar sights in the sky as the easiest gateway to the universe for young children. The activities she has designed pique the curiosity of youngsters about space and introduce them to the related vocabulary.

Most importantly, Joanne does not merely give the children information about space. She constantly relates this knowledge to their personal lives. In these, their most impressionable years, Joanne constantly urges her students to care for Planet Earth, and to be open to its wonderful fabric of diversity.

This book will give readers passage into Joanne's classroom. Here they can pause, absorb the details and feel the excitement of discovery with the three through six year-olds. They can also visualize how these activities are equally appropriate for seven and eight year-olds. It is my hope that Joanne's sharing will inspire many teachers to introduce young children to the unique elements of Planet Earth as well as to the wonders beyond its boundaries.

Aline D. Wolf

December 2002

[1]Described in *Children of the Universe, Cosmic Education in the Elementary Classroom* by Michael and D'Neil Duffy.

Foreword

My classroom has always been a window on the world for both my students and myself. On the shelves are all the traditional Montessori materials. The children use them regularly as they lengthen their concentration, sharpen their powers of observation and take those important early steps in math, reading, and geography. To the children these materials offer the gifts of calmness and joy in learning, as each one proceeds naturally at his or her own pace.

Strengthened by these gifts, the children and I, together, have always looked beyond our classroom walls. We explore and treasure all the wonders of nature found outside our school and we make special efforts to meet both children and adults from cultures other than our own.

After I attended International Space Camp, I realized that space was a new frontier to probe with the children. Like most adults today, I can't begin to imagine the developments in space that will define the 21st century, but I feel called to give some basic preparation to my students for what they are likely to experience in their future.

To do this I had to enlarge our window on the world to include the solar system and what lies beyond it. As I began this work I relied heavily on my knowledge of the children's concrete level of thinking and of their ability to wonder at the world around them. I had seen these primary students watch and wait patiently for a butterfly to emerge from its chrysalis after thirty minutes of effort. I wanted them to feel the same kind of amazement about what we could discover together about space.

Also, I had been impressed many times by their eagerness to know the names of things in nature. One year we could not find a monarch caterpillar, but in the process of looking for one, we discovered thirteen different larvae around our school. To identify these, the children wanted me to immediately find a guide book for caterpillars and insects. I did, and through the process we all became better informed. Would they also want to know the names for the wonders in space? I felt they would, so I thought about how this could be achieved.

My goals for this project became:
- To help the children feel their connection to the universe.
- To nourish their awe and wonder for its mysteries.
- To introduce them to the components of the universe, especially our own solar system.
- To share with them some of the details and excitement of voyages into space.

- To enable the children to realize that the ground they stand on is Planet Earth – one of the nine planets that are constantly traveling around the sun.
- To help the children learn to care for the Earth – the only planet in our solar system that we presently know has life.
- To help the children respect Planet Earth as a community of many different people, plants and animals who must live peacefully together, because even as we stand in our classroom, we are connected to the world around us, not only on our street but beyond the oceans as well.

I thought of what Maria Montessori had urged in *To Educate the Human Potential*, "Let us give the child a vision of the whole universe…for all things are connected with each other to form one whole unity." These words, written before man ever ventured into space, became particularly relevant to me, as I pondered what kinds of classroom activities Montessori would have devised for the 21st century, if she were still alive.

I knew that she wanted children to observe carefully and to notice similarities and differences. She wanted them to associate appropriate names with the new things they discovered in their environment. Her materials, such as the three-part language cards, taught facts rather than fiction, so that the children would be firmly rooted in reality with knowledge they could recollect easily in their later education.

The students in my class, like most children today, had a variety of conflicting ideas about aliens and space travel that they had gleaned from movies, TV cartoons, and space toys. They had no means of distinguishing facts from fantasy. I wanted to use projects that would guide them into reality and give meaningful answers to their questions.

The activities that I will describe on the following pages can be used gradually throughout the school year, or compressed into a special unit of study that is in the classroom for five to six weeks. Materials for these activities can be placed in a specific area of the classroom, perhaps a cosmos corner. For each activity, I have suggested related books that you can read to the children or that they can look at themselves. The publishers of these books and addresses for ordering materials are found in the "Appendix" section.

Do not be overwhelmed by the number of activities and resources presented here. Begin with just a simple exercise such as the Star Bag. As the children become interested and ask questions, add other appropriate activities. You will enjoy learning new concepts with the children, as I did, and you may be inspired to create projects of your own.

Joanne Alex
December 2002

Observing the Familiar

Exploring the Schoolyard

In her book, *Nurturing the Spirit in Non-Sectarian Classrooms,*[2] Aline Wolf says that, "Interesting discoveries are often made, not when we have new landscapes to look at, but when we have new eyes to look at what we see everyday. Fostering children's sense of wonder means helping them to slow down and to linger in their observations of all that surrounds them." And so we begin with observations.

I like to divide my class into small groups of three or four children for exploring our schoolyard. I give each group a card with a picture of the area they are to explore outdoors – a log, a fence, a tree, a bush, a rock, the sky. Each group looks for growing things (flowers, moss, weeds, seedlings, clover, etc.) or moving things (ants, birds, worms, spiders, caterpillars, clouds, etc.) When we did this, one child in the group with the sky card spontaneously laid flat on his back and said, "I know the best way to look at the sky." He did and the others in his group joined him for a more detailed look at what had always been above them.

There are two simple tools that the children can make to help them investigate their surroundings – a Nature Scope and/or Binoculars. Either of these will narrow their field of vision and help them to focus on one object and its details. The children are much more serious about their explorations when they are using these props. After we explore, each group tells the class what they have observed. This activity can also be done on a nature walk.

Another fun activity is to play the "I Spy" game outdoors. You and the children can take turns saying, "I spy something that is..." The description can relate to color, size, shape, movement, etc. The other children then guess what the object is.

[2]Parent Child Press Inc., 1995. p.75

TOOLS

Nature Scope – A paper towel tube that the child can decorate by painting it or by placing leaves or petals on clear contact paper and wrapping it around the tube, leaving both ends open. Use with one eye closed.

Binoculars – Put two toilet paper tubes side by side and hold them together with a rubber band. Use a paper punch to make a hole on the outside edge of each tube and tie a string through them so that a child can hang them around his neck.

BOOKS

Backyard Insects
by Millicent Selsam and Ronald Goor

Somewhere
by Jane Baskwill

I Am an Artist
by Pat Lowery Collins

In the Woods:
Who's Been Here?
By Lindsay Barrett George

★★★★★

Dreams by Peter Spier
The Cloud Book
by Tomie de Paola
The Sky Tree
by Thomas Locker
It Looked Like Spilt Milk
by Charles G. Shaw

Daytime Sky Awareness

Ask your class, "How many of you saw the sky this morning?" Usually all will raise their hands. Then ask them to draw what they saw using crayons or colored pencils. When they have finished, take all your students outside to lie on their backs and look more carefully at the sky. **Be sure to remind the children not to look directly at the sun.** Is the sun shining brightly or covered with clouds? Is the sky blue? White? Grey? Almost black? Are there many clouds? A few clouds? Or no clouds? Can you see the moon? After they have observed carefully, ask them to draw the sky again and compare their new drawing with their first one. This activity shows children how to look more carefully at the details in the sky.[3]

Observing the Night Sky

The dazzling night sky, with an ever-changing moon and thousands of stars that are visible to the unaided eye, is totally different from the daytime sky that the children can observe during school time. Some teachers schedule a night sky watch for the children, but this is often disappointing when rain or clouds diminish visibility. Instead I use a Star Bag that each child, in turn, takes home to use in making his own observations. If you are compressing these activities into a five or six week unit, make several Star Bags so that each child can have a turn during the cosmos unit.

Taking home the Star Bag.

[3] The source for this activity is For Spacious Skies, 111 Brickyard Road, Athol MA 01331

The child who takes home a Star Bag waits for a clear night and then goes with one or both parents to a dark area away from city lights. First they look for the moon. Is it a full moon, a half moon, or a crescent moon? Is it high or low in the sky? Or is there no moon at all? Do they see any moving objects—an airplane, meteor, comet? Tell the children that a meteor looks like a trail of light that races across the sky and then disappears. It is also called a "shooting star." A comet, which also has a tail of light, is much larger and further away, so it appears to be moving slowly. It is a luminous heavenly object that can be seen for several nights when its orbit brings it close to the sun.

BOOKS

Our Stars
by Anne Rockwell

The Stargazers
by Gail Gibbons

The Night Sky
by Alice Pernick

Next they use the flashlight to look at the sky chart and then try to find similar configurations in the sky. The children may see thousands of twinkling stars in the sky. Do they see any that shine but do not twinkle? Do they see a fuzzy white band across the sky? (Milky Way) When they return home either the child or a parent writes in the star journal, giving the date and a short description or drawing of what they observed. The next day the child returns the Star Bag and tells the class what he saw in the sky.

There are two advantages to this procedure. First, the child will be motivated to look at the sky several times as he waits for a clear night. And second, best of all, he can enjoy this exciting experience with a parent – resulting possibly in continued discussion and further plans to look at the sky together.

Contents of the Star Bag.

Looking *"Out"* at the Stars

BOOKS
I Look Out at the Stars
by Aline D. Wolf

To help the children understand that the stars are all around Planet Earth, make a tiny clay figure of a child. Place the figure, lying on its back, on your area of North America on the classroom globe. Say, "This is one of you children lying on Planet Earth and looking *up* at the stars."

Then take a similar figure and place it at the tip of South America. Tell the children, "Here is a child in South America. Is he looking *down* at the stars?"

"No." Explain that both children are looking *out* at the stars because the stars are all around Planet Earth.

Using the classroom globe.

Star Activities in the Classroom

Making a Felt Night Sky

Making a Felt Night Sky.

BOOKS

Zoo in the Sky
by Jacqueline Mitton

The Big Dipper
by Franklyn M. Branley

Find the Constellations
by H.A. Rey

*Tales of the
Shimmering Sky*
by Susan Milord

*They Dance in the
Sky-Native American
Star Myths*
by Jean Guard Monroe and
Ray A. Williamson

Keepers of the Night
by Michael J. Caduto and
Joseph Bruchac

For this classroom activity use one yard of wide black felt as a background and hang it against a wall at the child's eye-level. From other colors of felt, cut out objects such as planets, sun, moon, meteoroids, rockets, space shuttles, stars, comets, etc. Put a basket of these objects near the felt background and have the children create their own night sky.

Introducing Constellations

Tell the children that for thousands of years the stars have fascinated people on Planet Earth. During most of these years there was no electricity or television, so at night they would spend many hours imagining that a particular group of stars resembled animals or other familiar objects. These groups of stars are called constellations.

Learning the patterns of the constellations will help children to recognize them on their own when they look at the sky on a starry night. Three-part language cards are an excellent

MUSIC

With the children sing *Twinkle, Twinkle Little Star* and give them the note pattern to play it on the Montessori bells, a keyboard or a xylophone.

tool for illustrating a few familiar constellations visible in your area. Make two cards for each constellation. On both cards put a diagram of the constellation. Below the diagram put the name of the constellation and the name of its related animal or object. Cut the names off the first card so that the child can do the activity of matching the name to the appropriate diagram, using the second card (featuring

both the diagram and the names) as a reference. Patterns of the constellations can be found in many science or astronomy reference books. (See Resources for Teachers)

Another material that the children particularly enjoy using is a set of constellation cards with overlays. Each base card has a constellation of stars. Each overlay has the figure of a corresponding animal or object drawn to match a constellation. Constellation Overlays are available from the company "in-print for children."

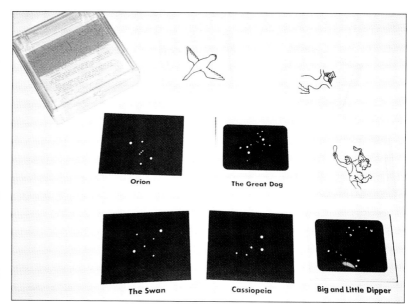

Some of the Constellation Overlays.

HOW TO MAKE THE PATTERNS

Use a constellation reference book and copy about four or five star patterns that are visible in your area, each on a separate white paper. Connect the stars with pencil lines so that the children can see the shape of the constellation.

Making Stars on Black Paper

On one of your shelves, place a tray that holds a small carpet sample, a piece of black construction paper the same size as the carpet sample, and a pushpin. The best pushpins are the large commercial-size or you can use round toothpicks. Show the children how to place the construction paper on the carpet sample and to punch small holes in the paper with the pushpin or the toothpick. Then hold the paper up to a bright light so that the holes look like stars twinkling in the night sky.

Next you can make plain white paper patterns of some of the familiar star formations, such as The Big Dipper,

The Little Dipper, Draco the Dragon and Orion. Lay the patterns, one at a time on top of pieces of the black paper and punch through both of these. When held to the light, each piece of black paper now shows one of the constellations of stars. Instead of the carpet sample, many teachers prefer to use a Lite Brite® (available in toy stores) for this activity.

If one of these patterns is made in the center of a small (3" x 3") piece of black paper, it can be taped to one end of the child's Nature Scope. (see pg. 1) The child can then get a sense of looking at a constellation through a real telescope.

Using a Lite Brite® to look at patterns of Constellations.

Looking at a star pattern through a Nature Scope.

Introducing Galaxies

Tell the children that there are so many stars in the universe that no one has ever been able to count them. There are more than thousands, more than millions, more than billions, even more than trillions. A very large group of stars is called a Galaxy. The name of our Galaxy is the Milky Way and it has more than a hundred billion stars.

On a clear night we can see part of our Milky Way Galaxy. It looks like a wide fuzzy band of tiny stars—almost like a milky streak across the sky. Perhaps some of the children have seen it when they took home the Star Bag and looked at the night sky with a parent.

To give the children an idea of what the Milky Way looks like you can do this fun activity. Use a 4" X 11" strip of dark blue or black paper. Place this paper around the inside of a quart yogurt container or a one pound coffee can. Take a ping-pong ball and put it into a jar or can of white or yellow paint, scoop it out with a plastic spoon and place it in the container with the paper. Put the lid on the container and shake or roll it around. When you open the container remove the paper and while it is still wet place it, paint side up, on the table and sprinkle the page with gold or silver glitter. This activity will give the children a replica of the band of stars we see across the sky, which is part of our Milky Way Galaxy.

Using a Classroom Planetarium

For a homemade planetarium, use a round oatmeal box. Punch a star pattern in the top cover, or remove the top cover, punch a variety of star patterns on individual pieces of black construction paper and tape them, one at a time, over the top of the oatmeal box. Remove the bottom cover and place the container over a regular flashlight to project the star pattern in a small dark space. A great dark space for this activity in your classroom is a pup tent in which one or two children can project the images on the interior of the tent. Because the interior of the tent must be very dark, it is best to cover the tent with a dark colored blanket or sheet. As an alternative you can purchase a home planetarium for this activity.

SOURCES FOR HOME PLANETARIUMS

Uncle Milton
Discovery Stores
Educational Design Inc.
Great Exploration
Scholastic Book Club

The Sun—Our Nearest Star

Tell the children that there is only one star that we can see in the daytime. "Does anyone know what it is?" Hint: "It looks much bigger and brighter than all the other stars." "Do you know why?" "It is much closer to us than any other star." At least one child, but usually more than one, will say, "It's the sun!"

The sun is our own special star. It is a huge ball of very hot gasses, always burning in an enormous blazing fire that is one million times bigger than Planet Earth! If you have made a Million Cube for your classroom you can compare it in size to a single Golden Bead, showing the children how much bigger the sun is than planet Earth.

Appreciating the Gifts from the Sun

The sun is constantly giving us gifts for life. Ask the children if they know what some of them are.

Light – Without the sun we would have darkness all the time, and nothing would ever grow. The following is an experiment to show how light is essential for growth. Plant bean seeds in two separate containers. Place one on a sunny windowsill and the other in a closed dark place in your classroom, such as a drawer that is kept closed. Water them equally on the same days of the week. Let the children monitor them for growth. Did the sun make a difference? Talk about how light is necessary for growing our food – vegetables and fruits as well as other trees and flowers.

A fascinating object to use to study light is a prism made of transparent glass consisting of various geometric shapes. Place the prism on a tray with a white felt mat. When a child chooses to work with the prism, he carries the tray to a sunny place in the classroom. The sun, shining through the prism, will then create a rainbow on the white felt mat. Will the colors remain on the white mat if the child carries it to a non-sunny place? Experiment! Will the colors be in the same order when it is returned to the sunny spot? Where do the colors come from? Explain that all the colors are in the light from the sun. The prism breaks down the light into separate colors that are in a special order. This rainbow of colors is called "the spectrum." Children

HOW TO MAKE A MILLION CUBE

Take six pieces of cardboard, each 30"X30" and tape them together to form a cube. Use your Thousand Cubes to show the children that the Million Cube is equal to 10 Thousand Cubes in length, 10 Thousand Cubes in width and 10 Thousand Cubes in depth.

BOOKS

The Sun is My Favorite Star by Frank Asch

Sun by Susan Canizares

★★★★★

Day Light, Night Light, Where the Light Comes From by Franklyn M. Branley

A Rainbow of My Own by Don Freeman

A Rainbow All Around Me by Sandra L. Pickney

SOURCE

A prism is available from Michael Olaf: *Child of the World Catalog*

love rainbows and often put them in their drawings. With the children, draw a beautiful rainbow for your classroom, putting the colors in the order of the spectrum that they see on the white felt mat. Hang a prism or crystal in a sunny window and watch the rainbows dance on the walls.

What makes the rainbow that we see in the sky when the sun is shining and it is raining at the same time? Tell the children that the raindrops act as prisms that break down the sunlight into its beautiful colors. The colors form the rainbow that we can see in the sky. A jar of water can be used to create a spectrum to demonstrate how rain forms a rainbow.

Gifts from the sun.

SOURCES

A Basic Solar Kit and Solar Oven are available from Carolina Catalog.

A sundial can be purchased from Montessori Services

A QUESTION TO PONDER

If the sun doesn't move, why does the shadow move?

FOLLOW-UP ACTIVITIES

Have each child make a booklet of the gifts of the sun. Have your group make a poster of these gifts.

BOOKS

Sun Calendar
by Una Jacobs

Nine O'clock Lullaby
by Marilyn Singer

Heat – Without the sun our whole planet would be very cold. No one could live here. To give the children more awareness of the heat from the sun, take a small group outdoors on a sunny day. Blindfold the children, one at a time, and lead them to a sunny spot and then to a shady spot, or vice versa. Let each child feel the temperature change and tell the group when she is in the shade and when she is in the sun. This activity enables the children to realize that the warmth that they often take for granted is a gift from the sun.

You and the children can also bake a simple recipe in a solar oven without using any gas or electricity. The solar oven must be placed directly in the hot sunlight. Baking brownies in this way takes about an hour.

Tell the children that solar panels are a special means of collecting heat from the sun. The children may have seen these panels on the roofs of nearby houses or buildings. If there are no solar panels in your neighborhood use photos. Explain that these panels can collect heat from the sun to warm the building or heat the water without using gas, oil or electricity that often pollute our environment.

Energy – The sun also gives us energy that can make things move. To demonstrate this, you will need a Basic

Solar Kit that contains a solar cell, a small motor and several propellers. Mount the motor on the edge of a board. The board will increase its durability and ease of use by a child. Put the board with the motor, the solar cell and the propellers on a tray on a classroom shelf. The child takes the tray to a sunny area and attaches one of the propellers to the motor. If she faces the solar cell toward the sun, the propeller will spin. When she moves it away from the sun, or covers the cell with her hand, the spinning stops. What does this exercise tell her about the sun? The children love to do this activity.

Time – For thousands of years the sun has helped us to keep track of time. The first clock was actually a sundial. A sundial has numbers in a circle like the clock in our classroom (not a digital clock), but instead of two hands, it has one upright or angled piece that casts a shadow toward one of the numbers in the circle. Position your sundial by turning it until the shadow points to the actual hour of the day as shown on your watch. When the sundial is

Using a solar cell to move a propeller.

correctly positioned the shadow will point to each hour of the day as the sun moves across the sky. For example if the shadow points on or near ten, it is about ten o'clock.

We have a portable sundial that can be used either in the classroom or outside. The children can position it in the morning and check throughout the day to see how it indicates the passage of the hours.

If you don't have a sundial you can place a stick or a pole upright in the ground in an open sunny area. In the morning of a sunny day, have the children place a marked stone on the tip of the shadow. When they return to the playground a few hours later, have them check to see if the shadow is still on the marked stone or has it moved to a different location.

Rotating Like the Earth—Showing Day and Night

Children sometimes ask, "Where does the sun go when it sets?" Or "Who turns the sun off at night?" To help the children to understand that the change from day to night is caused by the rotation of Planet Earth, I use the following activity. First I teach them the meaning of the word *rotate;* it means to turn completely around. To reinforce this definition, I ask

BOOKS

I Know the Sun Does Not "Set"
by Aline D. Wolf

Sun Up, Sun Down
by Gail Gibbons

What Makes Day and Night
by Franklyn M. Branley

each child, one after the other, to rotate, that is to stand up facing the window and to turn slowly around until facing the window again. Next I show them the globe, which is our map of the world, and I slowly rotate it completely around on its stand.

Then I light a table lamp with the lampshade removed, to represent the sun shining its light in all directions. I select one student to represent the Earth. He stands with the sun's light shining on his face and then slowly rotates so that the light gradually shifts to his back. When he completes the rotation the light shines on his face again.

Next I exchange this child for the globe that I place on the table with the lamp. Then I ask another student to rotate the globe very slowly toward the east. This shows the class that when the sun, represented by the lamp, shines on North and South America we have daylight. As the globe is slowly rotated, North and South America gradually move into darkness; the Pacific Ocean and then Asia face the sun and have daylight. Next Europe and Africa move into the path of the sun, then the Atlantic Ocean and when the rotation is complete, there is daylight again in North and South America. I constantly remind the children that the sun stays in the same place and is always shining. Instead of the Sun, it is Planet Earth that is rotating; and one complete rotation equals one full day.

The next time we look at our sundial, I ask the children, "If the sun doesn't move, then why does the shadow move around the clock?" Many of them say, "Because the Earth is rotating."

CHOICES OF BIRTHDAY BOOKS

On the Day You Were Born
by Debra Fraiser

Whoever You Are
by Mem Fox

What a Wonderful World
by Bob Thiele and George David Weiss

I Travel on Planet Earth
by Aline D. Wolf

A Birthday Walk Around the Sun

After the children become very familiar with the rotation of Planet Earth, I tell them that while it is rotating, Planet Earth is also traveling in its orbit as it makes a long journey around the sun. This journey takes one whole year. The tilt of the Earth as it travels gives us the seasons of spring, summer, fall and winter.

The birthday celebration of each child in the primary class is a wonderful parallel lesson illustrating the Earth's yearly journey around the sun. We have a special oval rug for this activity. In the center of the rug we place a beautiful wooden replica of the sun. Around the edge of the sun we place in order twelve cards on which are printed the names of the months. Starting with her month, a child

A birthday walk around the sun.

walks slowly around the rug carrying an inflatable globe of the Earth. The number of times she encircles the sun is equal to her age. For example, if she is five years old she goes around the printed twelve months of the year five times. This vividly illustrates the number of times the Earth has traveled around the sun since this child was born. To celebrate their special day, each birthday child brings a favorite snack to share with the class. This gives the child the experience of "giving" on her birthday as a complement to the usual receiving of gifts. She also shares a favorite book with the class that she chooses from our peace corner to be read aloud. After the reading we all sing *Happy Birthday*.

SOURCES

An inflatable globe is available from the National Geographic Society or in some local dollar stores. A wooden replica of the sun is available from Waseca Learning Environments.

ADDITIONAL OPTIONS

Invite the birthday child's parents to attend or to send a story from each year of the child's life that can be shared.

Make a video of the celebration for parents.

Our Solar System

If the children have been looking frequently at the night sky, they may have noticed that among the thousands of twinkling stars, there are a few bright lights that do not twinkle. The twinkling stars are balls of blazing gas, like our sun. The lights that do not twinkle are planets that are either made up of rocks, like Planet Earth, or are giant balls of cold gasses. They do not have their own light but reflect the light from the sun.

Scientists presently know of nine planets that orbit the sun in our solar system; five of them can be seen from Earth without a telescope—Mercury, Venus, Mars, Jupiter, and Saturn. Because the planets are constantly going around the sun, their position in the sky is always changing. Most are seen at different times; they are not all visible every night.

Singing About Our Planets

Singing songs about the planets is one of the best ways for children to learn the facts of our solar system. Here are some of our favorite songs:

Solar System Song[4]
(sung to the tune of "Yankee Doodle")

SUN
I am sunshine in the center
I am hot and burning
Life on Earth depends on me
So I must keep on turning.

Chorus

Round and round the sun we go
Never stop or slowing
Gravity pulls us around
So we must keep on going.

MERCURY
Mercury is made of iron
It is small and dusty
Hot in daytime cold at night
There's no air to be gusty.

VENUS
Venus is the next in line
The size of Earth, but drier
Poison gas keeps in the heat
It's hotter than a fire.

EARTH
Earth has water, air and land
Animals and plants too,
A moon that travels 'round each month
And weather we can live through.

MARS
Small and red and after Earth
Mars has many dust storms
The air is thin, the water's gone
There aren't any life forms.

[4]Donna Girard, used with permission

JUPITER

Jupiter the distant giant
Has a famous red spot
Moons are up to thirty-nine
Three rings are really not a lot!

NEPTUNE

Boasting strongest winds of all
And Great Dark Spot that's Earth-sized
Cold and dark and far away
Neptune is not a great prize.

SATURN

Seven rings of ice and rock
Surround the gaseous Saturn
Thirty moons go 'round it and
It glows just like a lantern.

PLUTO

Pluto makes the longest trip –
Two-hundred–forty-eight years
Smaller than the moon we know
A half-size Charon travels near.

URANUS

Twenty moons of Uranus
Travel 'round the sun too.
Each season lasts for many years
Eleven rings come shining through.

GRAND FINALE

Nine planets that we know about
And moons that orbit with them
Asteroids and meteors
Make up the Solar System!

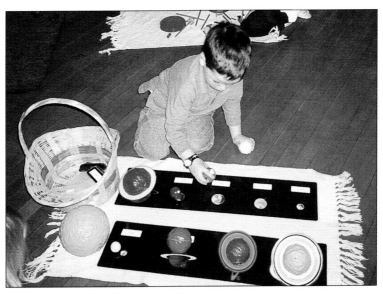

Naming a set of classrooms planets.

The Family of the Sun[5]

(sung to the tune of "The Farmer in the Dell)
Refrain

The family of the Sun,
The family of the Sun,
Here are nine planets in
The family of the Sun.

Mercury is hot
And Mercury is small.
Mercury has no atmosphere;
It's just a rocky ball.

Venus has thick clouds
That hide what is below.
The air is foul, the ground is hot;
It rotates very slowly.

We love the Earth, our home,
Its oceans and trees.
We eat its food, we breathe its air;
So no pollution, please.

Mars is very red;
It's also dry and cold.
Some day you might visit Mars,
If you are really bold.

Great Jupiter is big;
We've studied it a lot.
We found that it has many moons
And a big red spot.

Saturn has great rings;
We wondered what they were.
Now we know they're icy rocks
Which we saw as a blur.

Uranus and Neptune
We don't know much about.
Maybe we will study them
And then we'll all find out.

Pluto's last in line;
It's furthest from the Sun.
It's small and cold and icy too;
To land there won't be fun

Abby's Planet Song

(written by five year-old Abby Hannigan with her father when she was
a student at Stillwater Montessori School)

Mercury's the first planet from the sun,
Venus has choking clouds there isn't anyone,
Earth has mountains and oceans and trees,
Dogs and snakes and bumblebees.

Mars is red and has a mountain so tall,
Jupiter's the biggest planet of them all,
Saturn has rings that move so fast,
It's too bad that it has gas.

SOURCES FOR PLANET POSTERS

NASA Educational Products

Astronomical Society of the Pacific

[5]Melvin Zisfein and Robert Wolfe, National Air and Space Museum, Smithsonian Institution. Used with permission.

Uranus is the color of a bean,
Neptune never will be green,
Pluto is cold and far away,
But it has the shortest day.

All of the planets are so good,
They go around the sun, like they should
The planets on my wall, I can touch,
I love the planets oh so much!

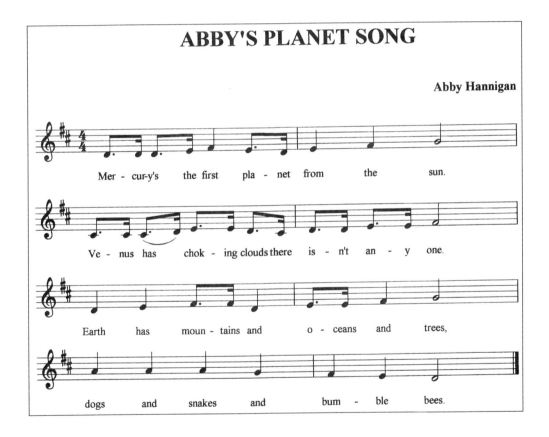

The children are usually excited to know that Earth has eight neighboring planets that get their light from the same sun as we do. These other eight planets travel around the sun, just as Earth does, but at different speeds and on different orbits or pathways. Nearly always the children will ask, "Do people live on the other planets?" And so we begin a series of activities that will introduce them to the prominent features of each of the planets. With this new information, the children begin to wonder if life as we know it could exist elsewhere. At this point a large poster of the planets in orbit is a useful visual aid.

Three-Part Language Cards for Planets

Make a set of three-part language cards for the planets in the same way you made three-part cards for the constellations. (See pg. 5) This exercise is a very effective way to help the children to associate the name of each planet with its picture.

Playing Concentration with the Planets

To reinforce their knowledge of the planets show the children how to play a game of Concentration with a set of matching cards. Spread out the cards face down on a rug. A child turns over one card and then a second one, hoping to find a match. If the two cards match, he removes them and starts his pile. If the two cards do not match, he turns them face down again and tries to remember their location for his next attempt. Two or three children take turns playing until all cards are matched. There are four ways to play Concentration, with gradually increasing difficulty:

Playing Concentration with the planets.

* Start with a set of cards containing two identical pictures of each planet.
* In a second set, match a picture of each planet with its name.
* In a third set, match a picture of each planet with a short description of it.
* In the fourth set, match the name of each planet with its description.

The "What Am I?" Game

This small group activity will also help children to learn the characteristics of the components of our Solar System. On a rug or a flannel board put a picture of each planet plus the sun and the moon. Then, from a set of cards that you have prepared, read a description of one of these and ask a student to find the picture that you have described. These are the descriptions I use for this activity:

I am a star. I can be found at the center of the Solar System and I am the star that is closest to the Earth. (Sun)

I am the closest planet to the Sun. I am the second smallest planet. I have no moons and when viewed through a telescope I appear to change shape from day to day. I have craters on my surface and I have hardly any air. (Mercury)

I am the brightest planet. I was named after the Roman goddess of love and beauty. I am also called the Evening Star and the Morning star. I am the second planet from the sun and I have no moons. Some people call me Earth's twin sister because we are about the same size. I am covered with thick clouds. (Venus)

I have been called "the ocean planet" because I am the only planet in the solar system with large amounts of water. I am the third planet from the sun, and I am the only planet known right now to have living things on it. A protective blanket called the atmosphere surrounds me. (Earth)

Playing the What Am I Game.

I am the fourth planet from the sun. I am named for the Roman god of war because of my red color. I have craters, mountains and valleys that are deeper and longer than the Grand Canyon. My surface is covered with an orange-red dusty soil. (Mars)

I am the largest planet. I am the fifth planet from the sun and I was named after the ruler of the Roman gods. I am made up of gases and covered by constantly moving thick clouds. I have more than 30

ANOTHER RESOURCE
Planetary descriptions in the Solar System Packet available from PaperCuts.

moons of different sizes. (Jupiter)

I am the second largest planet. I am
made up of gas and I have at least 1,000
rings around me. I was named after the Roman god
of farming, and I have more than 20 moons. (Saturn)

I am the seventh planet from the sun. I
am named for the Greek god of heaven
and ruler of the world. I have at least fifteen
moons and eleven rings. (Uranus)

I am too far from Earth to be seen without
a telescope. I am the eighth planet from
the sun. I am named after the Roman god
of the sea. I have two rings and at least
eight moons.   (Neptune)

I am the last planet in the solar system,
and also the smallest and coldest planet. I
have one large moon named Charon. (Pluto)

I am near the planet Earth. I am a barren
place with no water, no air, no clouds,
and no living things. I change the way I
look to you every day and these changes are called phases. (moon)

(Created by Heather Anzelc with information taken from *Our Solar System* by
Seymour Simon. Descriptions can be simplified for your group.)

The Planetary Walk

Children can get a more realistic idea of how the planets travel if nine of them walk the
orbits around the sun. Give each child a picture or a three-dimensional representation of one
of the planets.   Represent the sun with a lamp or with a picture of the sun. If you have
enough room, you can put masking tape on the floor to make the nine elliptical paths for the
children to follow. If not, just arrange the children in the planetary order. Mercury has the
orbit closest to the sun; Venus is next, then Earth, Mars, Jupiter, Saturn, Uranus, Neptune,
and finally Pluto. As the children walk the orbits they can sing: "The Planets Go Spinning."

When they sing the lines, "And they all go spinning, around and around they go," they can rotate a few times, as they walk on their orbits around the sun.

Getting ready for the Planetary Walk.

The Planets Go Spinning[6]

(Sing to the tune of "When Johnny Comes Marching Home.")

The planets revolve around the sun,
    hooray, hooray.
The planets revolve around the sun,
    hooray, hooray.
The planets revolve around the sun
And spin on their axes, every one.
And they all go spinning,
Around and around they go!

Mercury, Venus, Earth, and Mars,
    hooray, hooray.
Mercury, Venus, Earth, and Mars,
    hooray, hooray.

Mercury, Venus, Earth, and Mars,
All whirling and twirling among the stars.
And they all go spinning,
Around and around they go!

Jupiter and Saturn are next in line,
    hooray, hooray.
Jupiter and Saturn are next in line,
    hooray, hooray.
Jupiter and Saturn are next in line,
Uranus, Neptune, and Pluto make nine.
And they all go spinning,
Around and around they go!

TO MAKE A DRAWSTRING BAG

Choose a 9" X 12" piece of sturdy cloth.

Fold the top down 1 inch and sew to make a hem for the cord to go through.

String a 20" cord through the hem and tie the ends together.

Fold the 12" length of the cloth in half and sew up the bottom and side.

BOOKS

Postcards from Pluto, a Tour of the Solar System
by Loreen Leedy

The Planets in Our Solar System
by Franklyn M. Branley

The Magic School Bus, Lost in the Solar System
by Joanna Cole

Creating a Solar System to Take Home

There is an easy and inexpensive way to create replicas of the nine planets in sizes that are proportional to each other.

For Jupiter – a golf ball
For Saturn – a ping-pong ball
For Uranus – a large brown marble
For Neptune – a large blue marble
For Mars – a small red marble
For Earth – a small blue-green marble
For Venus – a small yellow marble
For Mercury – a silver seed bead
For Pluto – a white seed bead.

The seed beads are available in craft stores. Glue each seed bead on a small piece of construction paper to keep it from getting lost. Have enough of the above items for each child in your class. Help each one to make a drawstring bag in which they can carry home their planets. Give each child a card with the names of the planets and the objects representing them (as detailed above). If they have a large beach ball at home it will be approximately the right size to serve as the sun and they can place the planets around it. This project will enable the children to share the solar system with their families.

Planet Earth

As children learn the characteristics of the other eight planets, they begin to see why Planet Earth is very special. The planets closer to the sun have extremely high temperatures—much too hot for life as we know it. Those further from the sun are extremely cold and are made up of poisonous gases with no land or water. Mars, Venus and Mercury have land but no water and no life-sustaining atmosphere. Only Planet Earth has the right temperature and the necessary elements—Land, Water and Air—to support human life.
While doing the following activities, the children and I have frequent discussions about the importance of the elements. They already know why we need the fire of the sun, so I ask them, "Why do we need land?" "Why do we need water?" "Why do we need air?"

I put particular emphasis on air, which is not as evident to the children as land and water. To pinpoint the atmosphere I use my hands to encircle the globe about an inch or two away from its surface. I tell the children that between my hands and the globe of Planet Earth is the atmosphere. It has all the air that we breathe; it is where the birds, bees, kites and airplanes fly; it is where the wind blows; and it is our constant protection from the direct rays of the sun. Out beyond our atmosphere there is no air to breathe; there is only space.

The Element Tray

On my science shelf I have a tray with a paper on which I printed the three words—LAND, WATER and AIR. Beside each word is a jar representing that element. The LAND jar contains some topsoil and little stones. The WATER jar is half filled with water. The AIR jar looks empty but it is actually filled with air. The fourth element is Fire.

Although the sun is not an element of Planet Earth, it is comprised of the element Fire and its gifts of light and heat are essential for life. In order to represent FIRE, I put a small Styrofoam ball or a ping-pong ball painted yellow on the Element Tray to represent the ball of fire that is our sun. Beside it I print the word FIRE. The child using the tray removes the jars and the ball, mixes their order and then replaces each one beside the appropriate name.

For a separate exercise I have a basket of objects that serve as concrete

The Element Tray.

representations of the elements and the fireball. A small rock represents land; a seashell represents water; a feather represents air and a birthday candle represents fire. The children match these to the jars and ball used for the original presentation.

An Extension of the Birthday Celebration

Since a child's birthday celebrates life, it is also appropriate on that day to celebrate the elements that support his life. After the birthday walk (described on pg. 13) I place a rug in front of the seated birthday child. On it I put a ball made of blue and green modeling clay to represent the Earth. Then I hand him the tray of elements described above.

Together we sing, to the tune of *Twinkle, Twinkle, Little Star:*

> Earth of goodness helps you grow;
> Air of peace will gently blow;
> Fire of love, born to thee;
> Water of hope helps you see.
> (Child's name) you're a child of Earth,
> So we celebrate your birth.

(Shared by Amy Peterson-Roper)

While we are singing, the birthday child presses the rock, the shell, the feather and the

Pressing objects representing the Elements into a clay Earth ball.

candle into the ball of clay. When the clay dries, these objects will remain attached to the ball and the child takes his creation home as a reminder of the elements that support his life.

Sorting Animals—on Land, in Water, in the Air

Our work with the elements also includes the activity of sorting pictures of animals by how they travel—on land, in water or in the air. You can collect pictures of a horse, dog, cat, cow, bear, lion to be mixed with pictures of various fish and shellfish, birds, bees, flies, mosquitoes, etc., or you can order a commercial set. The child places each picture in a row beside the appropriate element jar. We understand that animals do not travel in fire.

SOURCE
Land, Sea, Air Exercise available from Priority Montessori.

BOOKS
Planet Earth Inside/Out by Gail Gibbons

How to Dig a Hole to the Other Side of the World by Faith McNulty

The Magic School Bus Inside the Earth by Joanna Cole

Tossing the Globe to Show Preponderance of Water

To help the children realize that there is more water than land on Planet Earth we use an inflatable globe that I toss to each child in the class. As each child catches it, we ask if his thumbs are on land or water. We keep a tally of all the responses and we soon see that there is a much bigger chance of having his thumbs on water, which helps us come to the conclusion that Planet Earth is covered with more water than land.

Molding the Layers of Planet Earth

Children often want to know what is under the surface of the Earth. Some of them say they are going to dig a very deep hole to see what they will find. Once a child asked if the water on one side of the globe went all the way through to the other side of the globe.

Joanne and her students molding the layers of Planet Earth.

Clay Recipe

2 cups water
2 cups flour
1 cup salt
2 teaspoons cream of tartar
2 tablespoons vegetable oil
    Food coloring.

Combine all ingredients, mix well and cook over medium heat, preferably in an electric frying pan. Stir constantly until clay forms a soft ball that is not sticky. Remove from heat and knead until it forms a smooth round ball.

For a Class of 20

Make one batch of red for center (form small balls for inner core)

One batch of yellow (form larger balls for outer core)

Two batches of orange (mantle)

One batch of green
One batch of blue
Combine a small piece of green and a small piece of blue to make outer crust.

When children ask such questions it is an ideal time to read them a book about the interior of Planet Earth.

After some reading and discussion I use clay to build a model that will help the children to visualize the various layers under the surface of Planet Earth. First I prepare four colors of clay for each child. As each child watches me, she builds her own model. It is a project that we all do together, and it is a favorite with the children.

First I take a small portion of red clay and form it into a round ball that is about one inch in diameter. I tell them that this represents the inner core of the Earth, which is solid rock.

Next I take the yellow clay ball, flatten it and wrap it around the red ball. I tell them that this represents the outer core that is mostly hot molten rock—that is, rock that is so hot that it has melted into a liquid.

Next I take the orange clay ball, flatten it and wrap it around the yellow clay. This is the mantle and it is solid with rocks much larger than those we see on the surface. Finally I take the blue-green clay ball, flatten it and wrap it around the orange layer to make the crust. This represents the Earth's surface of land and water.

After the children have completed their own models I hold up the completed blue-green model and ask the children, "How do we know that the layers are still under the surface?" To find out, we each take a piece of fishing line and slice through our models. All of the layers are revealed in each half. The children are always excited when they see the layers they have created. Some children enjoy making toothpick flags to label each layer—Inner Core, Outer Core, Mantle and Crust.

A student showing her inner layers of Planet Earth.

The Moon—A Traveler in Space

Most children are familiar with the word *space*. They have seen pictures of space men and spacecrafts. They know space is "out there" but they don't fully understand all that it entails. As we venture into the study of space, we start with the moon, which is our nearest neighbor in space. As far as we know it is the only other place in our solar system that human beings have touched.

Describing the Moon

Although the moon is familiar to children, it is difficult for them to understand why it always appears to be changing its shape. Some children think there are several moons that they can see on different nights—a great big moon, a half moon and a little sliver of moon. Others think that the moon is at first very tiny and then it blows itself up to a great big round dish.

What actually is the moon? I tell the children that it is a rocky sphere somewhat like Planet Earth only much smaller. They are surprised to learn that its color is not as it appears in the sky. The moon's surface is covered with a layer of charcoal-colored soil that varies from light to dark gray. It has no light of its own. At different times it appears to us to be varying shades of white, yellow, silver or orange as it reflects the very bright light of the sun. The moon also rotates on its axis, as the Earth does, so that it has daylight on the side that is facing the sun and darkness on the side that is away from the sun. However, the moon rotates much more slowly than the Earth, so each side of it has daylight equal to about two weeks of our time, followed by darkness equal to about two weeks of our time. I ask the children how they would like to stay awake for two weeks of daylight and then sleep for the two weeks of darkness.

The moon also goes around the Earth in the same way that the Earth orbits the sun. It takes one year for the Earth to go around the sun, but it takes only about one month for the moon to travel around the Earth.

Demonstrating the Moon's Phases

Every month while it is traveling around the Earth we see the moon in different shapes. In the lunar logs in our Star Bags we have records of when there is no moon, a crescent moon, a half moon and a full moon. The children, however, need a demonstration to help them to understand these different phases. I ask one child to represent the Earth and to hold a Styrofoam ball about the size of an orange that is mounted on a pencil or bamboo skewer. This Styrofoam ball represents the moon. A few feet in front of him on a shelf a little higher than his head, I place a gooseneck lamp (representing the sun). I darken the room in which the child is standing and he faces the lamp. The child holds the ball in front of him, raised slightly higher than his head. The lamp lights the side of the moon that is turned away from him, so the child sees only the unlighted side. This is called a new moon. It occurs once every month when we, on Earth, cannot see the moon at all.

As he turns gradually toward his right the light falls on a tiny portion of the ball and a sliver of the moon becomes visible. From Earth, and from the child's vantage point, it looks like a crescent. When he turns one quarter of the way around he sees a half moon. We say the moon is waxing, meaning that the lighted part is getting larger. When he turns half way around, the lamp representing the sun, is shining directly on the ball and he sees a full moon. As he continues

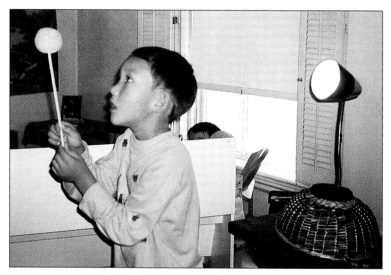

Looking at the full moon with his back toward the sun.

the light shines on smaller and smaller portions of the moon and we say the moon is waning—meaning that the lighted part is decreasing. When he is three-quarters of the way around, he sees another half moon; then a crescent moon. Finally when he is back where he started, we have another new moon, that we cannot see from Earth.

I give each child who is interested an individual chance to do this activity, because only the child holding the Styrofoam ball is able to see each of the phases as they are lighted by the lamp. The group of children watching are not in the right position to see the shape of the moon gradually changing.

On rare occasions the Earth passes directly between the sun and the moon. This causes an **eclipse**, which is the shadow of the Earth that partially or completely

Arranging the phases of the moon in sequential order.

covers the moon. In the above activity if the lamp (representing the sun), the child's head (representing Earth) and the ball (representing the moon) are in a direct line, all at the same height, the shadow of the Earth can be seen on the full moon. This demonstrates an eclipse of the moon. This phenomenon will particularly interest the children if one happens to occur during the school year, and you prepare the children to see it by doing this eclipse activity for several days prior to the announced date.

Looking at the Surface of the Moon

Since the moon is easier to spot than the constellations of stars, it is the most obvious night image to use for introducing the children to binoculars. However, before they use binoculars at night we practice using them in our schoolyard. The children are fascinated when they are able to use the binoculars to look closely at a bird's nest that is high up in a tree. Focusing binoculars on a particular object is not easy for children, so we practice looking at various objects.

Many families have binoculars at home that the children can use to look at the surface of the moon. Ask the children to describe what they have seen. They may say that the moon looks bumpy or rocky or that it has some parts that are light and some that are dark. Tell the children that looking from Earth we always see the same side of the moon. The only people who have seen the other side of the moon are astronauts who have traveled around the moon in a spacecraft.

Because the moon is so close to us, it looks bigger than the stars, but actually it is much, much smaller. If we look through a telescope we can see that the moon has high mountains, large valleys and deep craters. I tell the children that the moon has a rough, rocky surface and nothing grows there. It is perfectly quiet there. It has no air for anyone to breathe, no water to drink and no fertile soil where food can grow. Its nights are bitterly cold and its days are unbearably hot.

Encourage the families of your students to take a walk on a night when the moon is full; or organize one with your class. Use the binoculars to study the surface of the moon. Enjoy what is happening around you as you walk on Earth under the moonlight. Make sure to notice the moon shadows and any nighttime activities of nature.

SOURCES
Moon posters are available from The Astronomical Society of the Pacific and from NASA.
Moon Phase Nomenclature is available from Priority Montessori.

BOOKS
The Moon Seems to Change
by Franklyn M. Branley

What The Moon is Like
by Franklyn M. Branley

★★★★★

Walk When the Moon is Full
by Frances Hammerstrom

SOURCES
Child-size binoculars are available from Discovery Toys.

Creating A Crater in the Classroom

I tell the children that the deep valleys that they see in the moon are craters. They are formed when meteoroids hit the moon. A meteoroid is a large rocky or metallic object that travels in space. When a meteoroid collides with the moon, the impact is so hard that it creates a deep valley that is called a crater. Throughout the ages many meteoroids have hit the moon.

The children may wonder what would happen if meteoroids ever hit the Earth. Large meteoroids have hit the Earth in the past, but now they collide with Earth less frequently because there is not as much large debris left in space. Also Earth is somewhat protected by its atmosphere. If a small meteoroid comes into the Earth's atmosphere it burns up as it travels across the sky and disappears. This is what we call a meteor or "shooting star." It does not form a crater on the Earth.

To demonstrate how craters are formed, take a rectangular plastic dishpan about 13" long, 5" wide and 6" deep. Put a 5 lb bag of white flour into it. After smoothing the flour until it is level, put some dry cocoa into a sifter and sift a thin layer of cocoa over the flour. Provide a few different rocks of various sizes (not too big for little hands) that

Showing how a crater is formed.

the children can drop into the bin from various heights. This activity will show them how a crater is formed when a meteoroid hits the moon. When a child is finished with this activity, he can smooth the surface of the flour and cover it with a new thin layer of sifted cocoa. The pan is then ready for another child to use.

BOOKS

Let's Go to the Moon
by Janis Knudsen Wheat
(National Geographic
Society Young Explorers
Series.)

The Moon Book
by Gail Gibbons

Meteor by Patricia Polacca

Rockets

Talking About Gravity

Some of the children may have heard that astronauts have actually visited the moon. This idea is exciting for them and they want to know "How did they get there?" and "Could they walk on the moon?"

Before we can answer some of these questions it is important that the children begin to understand gravity. Gravity is the mysterious power that holds everything and every person on the Earth. No matter how high the children jump they will always come back to the ground. If they let go of their pencil, it will not go up to the ceiling but will fall to the floor. We do many little experiments like this until the children are sure of the meaning of gravity. When they see how everything is pulled toward the Earth, they begin to understand how difficult it was for the astronauts to escape from Earth's gravity and go to the moon.

Demonstrating How Rockets Move

In order to make it possible for astronauts to get free from the very powerful pull of Earth's gravity, scientists developed powerful rockets. A rocket consists of a container of pressurized gas. When this is burned, the exhaust escapes with a tremendous force and propels the rocket forward. These rockets are so powerful that they can push a spacecraft beyond the Earth's atmosphere into space.

A demonstration with a blown up balloon can give children a sense of how a rocket works. The air inside the balloon is under pressure just like the gas that is inside a rocket. For the first part of the demonstration blow up a balloon, pinch the neck tight to hold the air in, raise the balloon into the air and let it go. What happens? The air released from the balloon moves it forward with unexpected force.

The children are usually surprised because the balloon zigzags around the room and doesn't make much progress in any one direction. I ask them if they think a rocket could travel all the way to the moon by zigzagging in that way. NO! It has to be guided on a straight path.

To illustrate how we can make the balloon go in a straight line, I take a piece of string about 25 feet long and tape one end to the wall about 6' from the floor. I put the other end of the string through a straw. Then I blow up a long thin balloon and hold the neck tight. I walk with the string to the opposite side of the room and hold the string taut near the floor. The string is now on a rising diagonal and the straw is near the floor. The children help me to tape the balloon on to the straw. Then I let go of the neck. The escaping air propels the straw and balloon forward in a straight line. The children are fascinated as the balloon seems to fly along the string. You can experiment with the string in a horizontal, vertical and diagonal position to see if the balloon rocket moves in the same or a different way.

BOOKS

I Know What Gravity Does by Aline D. Wolf

Space Vehicles by Anne Rockwell and David Brion

Regards to the Man in the Moon by Ezra Jack Keats.

This experiment tells us that rockets need to be guided. Scientists can't tie a string on the moon, so they use very small rockets to steer the main rocket that is pushing the spacecraft. When the burning rocket fuel releases gases, like the air coming out of a balloon, it propels the spacecraft forward. The rocket is millions of times larger than our little balloon. It is so powerful that it can push its way through the Earth's atmosphere and escape from the downward pull of the Earth's gravity.

Explain to the children that the rocket is used to push an attached spacecraft into orbit, either around the Earth or around the moon. After each stage of the rocket has done its work, it falls away from the spacecraft and disintegrates. The astronauts continue riding in the spacecraft, which can now orbit the Earth, or if propelled to the moon, it can then orbit the moon.

Although rocket power is a fairly advanced topic, the balloon demonstration can give children an idea of the basic principle on which it is based. Without the development of rockets, no one would have been able to travel into space.

Building A Classroom Spacecraft

In order to let the children have an imaginative journey around the Earth, you can create a cardboard spacecraft for your classroom. Use a washing machine box or a refrigerator box. Build a control panel inside using cereal boxes or other recyclables to make knobs and levers. Cut a window in one side of the large box. On a wall directly outside this window hang a large poster of objects in space or a felt universe (as described on pg. 5). The children can then look out the window at the planets and stars as they go on their imaginative journey into space.

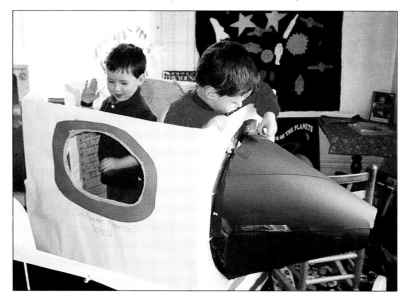

Our classroom spacecraft.

Imaginary trip in the classroom spacecraft.

Art and 3-D Construction

Primary students are usually not able to verbalize or write descriptions of what they have learned. However, in their art they usually can reflect some of the information they have acquired. It is important, therefore, to have art materials readily available for children to express their ideas and feelings.

During the time that we are talking about rockets, I keep a selection of children's books with pictures of spacecraft on a low bookshelf. Beside it, is a table of art supplies. In addition to the usual paper, colored pencils, markers, and crayons, I put a basket of paper towel tubes, empty yogurt containers, paper plates, glue sticks and other supplies that can be used for 3-D construction.

In this area I also include a set of Tinkertoys that have a wide variety of shapes, useful for creating a space vehicle. For more

Constructing 3-D rockets.

advanced students I have a Lego Kit with step-by-step instructions for constructing an actual model of the moon rover. I am always amazed at what the children create. I have learned never to underestimate their interest or abilities!

REFERENCES FOR BUILDING SPACECRAFT

Spacecraft
by Robin Kerrod

Space Craft
by Peter M. Spizzirri

Shuttle Craft
by Peter M. Spizzirri

Traveling in Space
by Sue Becklake

Building a moon rover.

Living in Space

Breathing

The atmosphere around the Earth provides the air that we breathe in order to stay alive. It is made up of oxygen and nitrogen. Many people notice that it is easiest to breathe at sea level, which is the level of the beach beside the ocean. If they climb a high mountain, they may get out of breath, because the air is thinner and has less oxygen at higher altitudes. Airplanes that travel more than two miles high must carry oxygen for the occupants to breathe.

The further one gets away from the Earth's surface, the thinner the atmosphere. At about 100 miles away from the Earth, the atmosphere fades away and there is only space with no air to breathe.

In order to breathe in space, astronauts must carry enough oxygen with them for their entire trip. The inside of their spacecraft has a controlled environment with the right amount of oxygen. If an astronaut goes outside the spacecraft, (e.g. to repair a satellite or to walk on the moon) he must carry a tank of oxygen so that he can breathe. Providing enough air for astronauts in flight is very important because without it they could not live.

Walking, Sitting and Working

As astronauts travel into space they gradually escape from the strong gravity that draws everything toward the Earth. The gravity they experience becomes weaker and weaker until they are only slightly affected by what we call micro-gravity. This means that every person and every object within an orbiting spacecraft will float around in the air. Ask the children if they can imagine an astronaut who cannot stay seated in his chair unless he is strapped into it? Food that will not stay on the table? Papers and books that constantly float around the room? If an astronaut wants to go to another area of the spacecraft, he cannot walk there. He must use handholds and footholds attached to the wall and ceiling to push himself as he floats to where he wants to go. Also the cabin of a spacecraft has a lot of Velcro, clips, magnets and drawers to keep things like dishes, toothbrushes, pencils, and silverware in their designated places. To give your students an actual picture of this, have them watch *Living in Space*, a video showing how the astronauts actually live and work.

Playing With Toys

We, who are living on Earth, take gravity for granted; we hardly ever think about it. Only when we realize what life is like with only micro-gravity, can we appreciate all that gravity does for us everyday. Toys in Space is a fun activity that gives children a chance to predict how their toys would perform in space, where there is only micro-gravity. For this activity you need the video *Toys in Space II*. First I set up a basket with some of the toys that are featured in the video, such as a Slinky®, Klackers, Magnetic Balls, and a Jacob's

Ladder. After the children play with the toys, I ask them how they think these toys would perform in space where there is only micro-gravity. They guess whether it would be the same or different to play with each of the toys in space. We keep a simple chart of their responses – Same or Different – and then we watch the video to see which predictions were correct.

Wearing Special Clothes

An astronaut has special clothes for inside the spacecraft and special clothes for outside the spacecraft. A one-piece flight suit is what most astronauts wear when working inside the spacecraft. A flight suit has pockets with Velcro and zippers and has loops to hold pencils and other gear. When an astronaut needs a notebook, she may use a kneeboard instead, which straps around her leg and acts as a writing surface.

When going outside the spacecraft, an astronaut must wear a special suit and backpack that together create an independent life support system. This provides all the necessary supplies for the astronaut to live. The backpack is called a Portable Life Support System that carries oxygen and water for the astronaut to use. This backpack is connected by special hoses to the astronaut's space suit.

Eating and Drinking

The children are well aware that no one can live without food and water. What do astronauts eat and drink where there are no grocery stores, no fertile land to grow food, and no wells or reservoirs for water? The answer, of course, is that they must bring all their food and drink with them in their spacecraft. Since the spacecraft is small, they must select nourishing foods that take up a minimal amount of room.

Some foods can go into space in their natural form, such as candy, nuts, cookies, crackers, granola bars and peanut butter. Others, such as fruits, must be freeze-dried or dehydrated in order to weigh less and last longer.

To demonstrate the dehydration process, use two apples of equal size. Set aside one apple. Cut the second apple into slices. These slices can be dried in a dehydrator, if you have one. If not use a needle to put them on a string and hang them in your classroom. When they are sufficiently dried, compare the slices with the fresh whole apple. Have one child hold out her hands, palms up. Put the fresh apple on one hand and the equivalent dried slices on the other. What does she notice? Which apple would be more suitable for space travel?

Foods that crumble easily present another problem in space, because the crumbs can easily float into sensitive equipment and cause serious damage.

Ask the children which would be a better choice for space – saltine crackers or bite-size snack crackers, such as wheat thins. After they have given their opinions, give each child a saltine to eat over a napkin. Did any crumbs fall on the napkin? Then give them a bite-size cracker and compare the results.

Astronauts do not have to bring a large supply of water with them when they journey into space. Fortunately water is the by-product of the fuel cells on the spacecraft and is always available. They reclaim and reuse as much water as possible.

Since water is so readily available, astronauts bring powdered drinks such as cocoa, powdered milk, orange crystals, etc. to mix with water in their tiny kitchen area. It is difficult for them to drink from a glass because of micro-gravity, so astronauts must keep lids on their containers and drink the liquids through a straw at all times. There are also many dried foods, such as soups, that can be reconstituted by adding water.

To give children the experience of reconstituting orange crystals, set up a drink making activity in your snack area. The child puts a tablespoon of crystals in a five ounce (5 oz.) glass, adds water from a pitcher, stirs with a spoon, puts a plastic lid on the glass and, as the astronauts do, drinks with a straw that goes through a small hole in the lid.

Mixing crystals with water for a space drink.

Shopping for Space Travel

After talking about the astronauts' food the children can do this sorting activity that invites them to select foods that are suitable for space travel. Beside a large paper bag labeled "Shopping for Space Travel" I place a basket filled with a group of familiar grocery items.

ITEMS FOR SHOPPING FOR SPACE

Can of soup	Dehydrated packet of soup
Box of cold cereal	Individual packets of oatmeal
Fresh apple	Dried apple slices in a baggie
Bottle of juice	Individual packet of orange crystals
Box of macaroni and cheese	Pouch of dried macaroni & cheese
Can of beef	Beef jerky

Using the criteria of size and weight, the child examines each item and places those that are appropriate for space travel near a card with the word Space and those that are not suitable for space near a card with the word Earth. After the child has sorted the packages, cans, bottles and pouches, she puts the foods suitable for space into the grocery bag and the remaining items into the basket. This is a fun activity that reinforces some of the information the children have learned about space travel.

Shopping for space travel.

BOOKS
If You Were an Astronaut
by Dinah L. Moche

I Want to be An Astronaut
by Bryon Barton

A Day in Space
by Lord and Tolie Epstein

Imagining Aliens

Read
Is There Life in Outer Space?
By Franklyn M. Branley

When children ask if there are creatures living on other planets, I explain to them that no one has yet discovered other life forms in space. Then I turn the question back to them. "What do you think?" Usually they say that there might be strange looking creatures living on planets far, far away. So I provide art supplies for them to draw or create whatever they are imagining. I tell them that we use the word, *alien*, to describe a being that could live in space but is presently not known to us.

A child's imaginary alien.

Using Your Community

Connecting With Astronomy Clubs

Most cities, both big and small, now have Astronomy Clubs in which people who are interested in the sky sponsor lectures and sky watches. They often circulate useful information about phases of the moon, comets, the changing locations of planets, eclipses of the sun and moon and constellations that are clearly visible in the local area.

Members of these clubs are usually eager to share their information with children of any age. Sometimes they will bring a larger than average telescope to a school and give children the experience of looking at a distant object at close range. At other times they will invite children to join them at a night sky watch where their expertise can guide students to see formations in the sky that are of particular seasonal interest.

Visiting Planetariums and Observatories

Nearly all major cities have sizeable planetariums that feature programs for students of various ages. Smaller cities also have more modest planetariums that are excellent community resources. Many planetariums and observatories are connected to colleges and universities.

To give my students a special experience of the universe, I set up a visit to our local planetarium and to a university observatory on the same day. In preparation for our field trip, I invited a local astronomer to bring his telescope to our school and explain how it works. He set up the telescope in our schoolyard and each child had an opportunity to become accustomed to the eyepiece and to learn how to look through it at a particular object.

We then discussed our upcoming visit to a planetarium show called "Our Sky Family" that featured a look at our solar system and a visit to each planet. After we attended the planetarium show, an astronomy professor

Looking through a professional telescope.

from the university opened the observatory for us. The children were thrilled as each one had a turn to look through the huge telescope. For our group it was a magical trip because it fell on March 21, the Spring Equinox, and Venus was in the day sky. When we returned to school we created a class book in which each child made a page about our exciting experience. Our school also had a Family Star Party at our local university observatory. We planned an evening event, with activities for the families to do while waiting their turn to use the big telescope.

Looking at the sky during a visit to an observatory.

Being Part of the Universe

One of my goals in planning this whole curriculum was to help children to feel their connection to the universe. In a world where most children's orientation to life is television and its non-stop commercials, I feel that they have to know that they are a part of something much larger and more important than their everyday world. Their fascination with candy bars, game boys, play stations, soft drinks and name brands will eventually fade, but the importance of Planet Earth, the Solar System and the universe will remain as an anchor of wisdom in their lives. I want them to see that even as they sit in our classroom, they are part of much larger domains that they can always respect, explore and care about.

My Place in Space Activity

To help children to understand their connection to the greater scheme of things I designed an activity called My Place in Space. For this exercise I used ten nesting houses, and a small representation of a heart (available in craft stores) that can fit under the smallest house. Because the nesting houses are difficult to obtain, nesting blocks or containers can be used if you label each one with a name or illustration.

The ten nesting houses represent a series of environments, each one larger than the previous one. The purpose of the activity is to show each child that he or she exists in all of these settings at the same time:

1. Your classroom (the smallest house)
2. Your school (by name)
3. Your city or town (by name)
4. Your state (by name)
5. Your country (by name)
6. Your continent (by name)
7. Planet Earth
8. The Solar System
9. The Milky Way
10. The universe

To present this exercise, line up the houses or containers from smallest to largest on a rug. In front of them place the heart. Explain to the children that the heart represents all of us and we are here in this classroom. To show that we are in the classroom, place the smallest unit over the heart.

Next tell the children that while we are in the classroom we are also in (name) School. Then place the second house or container over the smallest one. Continue saying, "While we are in our school, we are also in (name of your city)." Proceed in this way until you place the universe as the last and largest house. Then lift up all the houses or containers together

SOURCE
Measure up containers are available from Discovery Toys.

BOOKS
Me and My Place in Space by Joan Sweeney

I Live in the Universe by Aline D. Wolf

My Global Address by Tamara Nunn

From Here to There by Margery Cuyler

My Place in Space by Robin and Sally Hirst

★★★★★

Pledge to the Earth by Aline D. Wolf

The Earth and I by Frank Asch

Old Turtle by Douglas Wood

and tell the children, "We are in all these places at the same time; we are in our classroom and we are also in the universe.

For older children the activity can be done in reverse, beginning with the universe, as Montessori did. Start with all the houses or containers stacked and remove them, one by one, until the heart is found under the smallest one.

This activity shows the interconnectedness of all places in the universe and demonstrates that where we are and what we do affects all the other places. The children gradually begin to realize that we all share Planet Earth and after learning about the other planets they know that, at this point in time, it is the only place where we can live. Have each child draw a picture of her favorite place in the universe. Compile these pictures in a class booklet, in which you can record each child's verbal description of the place she likes best.

Becoming Stewards of the Earth

As the children journey through the universe in all these activities, they gradually realize that Planet Earth is very, very special. It is the only planet we know of, that has the elements we need to support life—fertile land, sufficient water and air that creatures can breathe. While these elements are common here on Earth, they do not exist in other parts of the universe that have been explored. We who benefit from them now must take good care of them, so that they will enable our children and grandchildren to live on Planet Earth in the future.

Protecting Planet Earth is everyone's job. Carelessness has already polluted large portions of our land, water and air so that it is getting more difficult for Planet Earth to support life. I tell the children, while they are at a very impressionable age, that they must be good stewards of the Earth. That means they must take care of it by reducing waste, reusing materials and recycling trash for future use.

In our classroom we had a project in which we saved all the trash generated for several days in our classroom. As we sorted through it, we found that paper products were the largest portion of what we were putting in a garbage dump that was polluting our land.

In order to reduce our paper waste we decided to use individual hand towels instead of paper ones, cloth napkins and hard plastic cups individually labeled for each child. We also gathered recyclable cans and bottles and sold them to fund such projects as the Children's

Rain Forest and our school field trips. All of these activities made the children very aware of the need to help Planet Earth.

Global Citizens Working for Peace

I also teach the children that as citizens of Planet Earth we have a responsibility to others with whom we share this Planet. In our geography lessons we learn about people whose language, religion, food, clothing, and homes are very different from ours. We also invite people from other cultures to visit our classroom and share some of their customs, holidays and celebrations. Some of the children have "Pals" in other countries to whom they send drawings, photos, notes and even videos. I constantly remind them that if we are to have peace in the world we must learn about other people and respect their appearance and ways of living that are different from ours.

Peace is vital to the survival of Planet Earth. Wars not only kill millions of people, they also pollute the air, water and land of Planet Earth. Perhaps the greatest lesson we can learn from this primary curriculum is that we must all be good Global Citizens who protect and care for Planet Earth—our very fragile home in the universe.

Our Peace Table

Children also have a great need for peace within themselves. To help them attain this, I have a Peace Table in a quiet corner of the classroom. Here one child at a time can

A selection of items for a Peace Table.

**TEACHERS'
RESOURCES FOR
PEACE**
Curriculum of Love
by Morgan Simone Daleo

Nurturing the Spirit
by Aline D. Wolf

*Peaceful Children,
Peaceful World*
by Aline D. Wolf

UNICEF Projects

Peace Packet from
PaperCuts

BOOKS
I Offer You Peace
by Aline D. Wolf

Peace Begins With You
by Katherine Scholes

Peace on Earth
by Bijou LeTord

The Butter Battle Book
by Dr. Seuss

Our Peaceful Classroom
by Aline D. Wolf

slip away from the general hubbub and spend a short time alone contemplating some gifts of nature or a beautiful object, such as a lovely plant or fresh flowers, a beautiful seashell, rock or a bird's nest in a tree outside the window. I also include some peace books and a globe of Planet Earth, inside of which are little dolls representing many different cultures in the world.

A Peace Table can also be used as a place where two children can come to resolve a disagreement. Here certain rules apply to the way they speak to each other. They express their feelings, one at a time, and try to peacefully find a solution to their conflict.

Evaluation of the Curriculum

I know that my cosmic curriculum is appropriate and meets the needs and interests of my students because on "share days" the children bring in "shares" related to space, which they have made, found, or created. Items they have shared in the past, include fabric with space prints, t-shirts with the planets on them, rockets, space shuttle models, handmade art work of solar systems, moons, rockets, a robot, books with pictures of the solar system and posters they bought or made. They are always excited to share these with our class. Also, the class books we made about space are their favorites to look at during the rest of the year.

Showing her poster of the planets and asteroids.

This curriculum answers many of the children's questions about "What's Out there?" It also gives them opportunities to ask more questions, as it speaks to their curiosity and sparks their wonder about the world around them. In our study of the solar system we begin to understand that our world is part of something much larger. Our solar system is a part of something even bigger called The Milky Way. The Milky Way is only one of many galaxies in our universe. "How many galaxies?" I wonder… All of this material prepares a fertile foundation for the 6 to 12 year-olds to participate in Montessori's unique Cosmic Education that may follow their years in the primary classroom.

In *Nurturing the Spirit in Non-Sectarian Classrooms*, Aline Wolf wrote, "If wonder becomes a fundamental attitude in a child's life it will confer on him or her a spiritual character, because wonder constantly reminds all of us of the mysteries of reality."[6] I know my cosmic curriculum prepares the children spiritually to begin to understand their place in the universe. If Dr. Maria Montessori were still living, I feel she would create such a curriculum herself, just as she developed her peace curriculum during the war years. This is the curriculum children need today in order to take their first steps to becoming world citizens. I hope that the work I have shared here will be a model, or springboard, for you as a teacher, to journey into the universe with your children and delight in the marvels that you will discover with them.

[6]Wolf, Aline D. Parent Child Press Inc., Hollidaysburg; p.87

Appendix

I want to know more.

Children's Books That Complement This Manual
(Some of these books have limited availability, but may be available in your local library.)

Observing the Familiar

Baskwill, Jane. *Somewhere*. Greenvale, NY: Mondo Publishing, 1996.
  Describes in verse and scratchboard artwork some of the many wonders of nature occurring around the world at one moment in time. The illustrations are very detailed.

Collins, Pat Lowery. *I am an Artist*. Brookfield, Connecticut: Millbrook Press, 1992. An artist helps us to see the natural beauty in the world around us.

dePaola, Tomie. *The Cloud Book*. New York: Scholastic Inc., 1975. This is an informational book on clouds written for children.

George, Lindsay Barrett. *In the Woods: Who's Been Here?*. New York: Scholastic Inc., 1996.

_____. *In the Snow: Who's Been Here?*. New York: Scholastic Inc., 1996

_____. *Around the Pond: Who's Been Here?*. New York, Scholastic Inc., 2000
  This series is beautifully illustrated and asks the child to guess from the clues/signs which animal has been there. Each answer is on the following page.

Gilbert, Joan. *Sense of Wonder Series*. Hollidaysburg, PA: Parent Child Press Inc., 1994. The stories are written so children can read them and think about the wonderful happenings in their world.

Lewis, Richard. *In The Space of The Sky*. New York: Harcourt Inc., 2002. A child's exploration of space, of the world and of dreams. The illustrations by Debra Frasier are exquisite.

Locker, Thomas. *Sky Tree (Seeing Science Through Art)*. New York: HarperCollins, 1995. Thomas Locker paints a tree through the seasons and notices its relation to the sky. This is a beautiful book to introduce art and observation skills to children.

Manning, Mick and Brita Granstrom. *What's Up?* New York: Scholastic Inc., 2002. Two children take you on a journey from earth to outer space by asking the question, "What's higher?"

Nail, Jim. *Who's Tracks are These?, A Clue Book of Familiar Forest Animals*. Boulder, Colorado: Roberts Rinehart Publishers, 1994. This is a book to help children look for signs and tracks and decide what animal made them. The realistic paintings of the animals are simple and clear.

Selsam, Millicent and Ronald Goor. *Backyard Insects*. New York: Scholastic Inc., 1981. This book encourages us to look closely at what insects we may find in our own backyards.
  _____, Big *Tracks, Little Tracks*. New York: Scholastic Inc., 1999. This book tells us how to read the signs and tracks we see.

Shaw, Charles G. *It Looked Like Spilt Milk*. New York: Scholastic Inc., 1989. It looks like milk but it is really a cloud in different shapes.

Showers, Paul. *The Listening Walk*. New York: The Trumpet Club, 1993. This book is a great read before taking a listening walk of your own. It reminds us to listen to the sounds in our environment.

Spier, Peter. *Dreams*. New York: The Trumpet Club, 1991. This is a wordless picture book that shows two children watching the sky and using their imaginations to see figures in the clouds.

Wolf, Aline D. *I Want to Hear the Quiet*. Hollidaysburg, PA: Parent Child Press Inc., 2001. We are reminded to listen to the quiet, within and without.

The Stars

Branley, Franklyn M. *The Big Dipper*. New York: HarperCollins Publishers, 1991. This book introduces looking for constellations with the star pattern of the Big Dipper. **Note:** Frank Branley, former chairman of the Hayden Planetarium in New York City, has written over 150 children's books on science, all clear and concise. Look for books by him.

Carle, Eric. *Draw Me a Star*. New York: Scholastic Inc., 1992.
Eric Carle's artwork is a delight as we learn how to draw a star.

Gibbons, Gail. *Stargazers*. New York: Scholastic Inc., 1992.
Gail Gibbons has used clear descriptions of stars and their relationship in the universe. Her book also talks about people who are star watching and looking for the constellations.

Mitton, Jacqueline. *Zoo in the Sky*. Washington, DC: National Geographic Society, 1998. This is a beautifully illustrated book of common animal constellations in the sky. The star patterns are in shiny foil to highlight the patterns seen in the night sky.

Pernick, Alice. *The Night Sky*. New York: Scholastic Inc., 1994. This story describes in simple text and beautiful pictures what one might see when the sun goes down.

Rey, Hans Augusto. *Find the Constellations*. Boston: Houghton Mifflin Company, revised edition 1976. This is a classic book with clear pictures of constellations and their history.

_____. *The Stars, a New Way to See Them*. Boston: Houghton Mifflin Company, revised edition 1976.
Rey has taken the constellation patterns and represented them in a graphic way rather than the traditional allegorical or geometrical ways. It simplifies the patterns for easier recognition.

Rockwell, Anne. *Our Stars*. New York: Silver Whistle, Harcourt Brace and Company, 1999. This book is a perfect introduction to the stars, our solar system and our universe. It has a simple text and clear illustrations.

Wolf, Aline D. *I Look" Out" at the Stars*. Hollidaysburg, PA: Parent Child Press Inc., 2000. With clear text and simple illustrations this little book shows how planet Earth is surrounded by stars and we all look "out", not up or down, to see the stars.

The Sun

Armstrong, Jennifer. *Sunshine, Moonshine*. New York: Random House, 1997. This is an early step-into-reading book about the sun and moonlight. A good choice for a beginning reader.

Asch, Frank. *The Sun is My Favorite Star*. Morristown, NJ: Silver Burdett Company, 1986. A child tells how the sun is important to her as she goes through her day from morning until night.

Branley, Franklyn M. *Day Light, Night Light, Where the Light Comes From*. New York: Scholastic Inc., 1998. Branley explains how the hot rays of the Sun are our main source of light.

_____, *What Makes Day and Night*. New York: HarperCollins Publishers Inc., 1986. In simple text and clear illustrations the author explains how the rotation of the earth causes day and night. A great book to read when you talk about the rotation of the earth with the children.

Canizares, Susan. *Sun*. New York: Scholastic Inc., 1998. This is an early reader with photographs and simple text about the light and heat from the sun. A page of information for adults to share with children is included in the back.

Dorros, Arthur. *Me and My Shadow*. New York: Scholastic Inc., 1990. Arthur Dorros explains what shadows are, including the shadows of the earth and the moon. The book includes simple experiments to do.

Freeman, Don. *A Rainbow of My Own*. Cedar Grove, NJ: Rae Publishing Co., 1978. A small boy imagines what it would be like to have a rainbow for a friend

Gibbons, Gail. *Sun up, Sun down*. New York: Scholastic Inc., 1992. A child observes the sun from morning until night asking her parents questions about it. The book has a simple, readable text and clear illustrations.

Jacobs, Una. *Sun Calendar*. Morristown, NJ: Silver Burdett Company, 1986. The text and illustrations follow the sun throughout a year and explain how the sun's position in the sky affects all life on earth.

Lindbergh, Reeve. *What is the Sun?* Cambridge, MA: Candlewick Press, 1994. This is a series of what and where questions asked by a child to a parent. The book starts with "What is the Sun?" and ends with a question about earth. The story is done in rhyming verse.

Pinkney, Sandra L. *A Rainbow All Around Me*. New York: Cartwheel Books, Scholastic Inc., 2002. This book combines the concept of the colors of the rainbow with photos of children from a broad multicultural background.

_____ *Shades of Black, A Celebration of our Children*. New York: Scholastic Inc., 2001. A book using photographs of children to show diversity. This book is a nice compliment to *A Rainbow All Around Me*.

Singer, Marilyn. *Nine O'clock Lullaby*. New York: Scholastic Inc., 1991. This book illustrates the rotation of the earth causing day and night. It shares with us what is happening around the world when it is 9:00 p.m. in New York.

Tabor, Nancy Maria Grande. *We are a Rainbow*. Watertown, MA: Charlesbridge Publishing, 1997. A child moving to a new country discovers that all people are more alike than different.

Wolf, Aline D. *I Know the Sun Does Not Set*. Hollidaysburg, PA: Parent Child Press Inc., 2001. This little book explains how the Earth's rotation makes the sun appear to rise and set.

The Solar System

Bendiek, Jeanne. *The Planets: Neighbors in Space*. Connecticut: The Millbrook Press Inc., 1991. This is a simple introduction to the planets.

Branley, Franklyn M. *The Planets in Our Solar System*. New York: Scholastic Inc., 1998. This is an excellent introduction to the nine planets and the Earth's special place in the solar system.

Cole, Joanna. *The Magic School Bus Lost in the Solar System*. New York: Scholastic Inc., 1990. The class travels on a magic school bus to visit each planet in the solar system. This is a favorite with the older students in my class.

Ford, Harry. *The Young Astronomer*. New York: Dorling Kindersley Inc., 1998. This is a helpful reference book for teachers that also includes projects. Children enjoy its detailed illustrations.

Gallant, Roy A. *National Geographic Picture Atlas of Our Universe*. Washington, DC: National Geographic Society, 1980. The illustrations and photos are excellent. This is another good resource book for teachers to use as well as for children to browse through.

Jeunesse, Galliniard. *The Universe*. (A first Discovery Book). New York: Scholastic Inc., 1997. This is a wonderful introduction to our solar system and the universe beyond. Students especially enjoy the overlay pages in the book.

_____ *The Earth and Sky* (A first Discovery Book). More wonderful overlay pages in this book from the perspective of Earth.

Leedy, Loreen. *Postcards from Pluto, A Tour of the Solar System*. New York: Scholastic Inc., 1995. A group of children tour the solar system and send home postcards from each planet with information about it.

Simon, Seymour. *Our Solar System*. New York: Morrow Junior Books, 1992. This book has excellent pictures and factual information about our solar system—the sun, the planets, moon, asteroids and comets.

_____ *Look to the Night Sky: An Introduction to Star Watching*. New York: Viking, 1977. This is a helpful resource for beginning stargazers looking at the sky without a telescope .

_____ *Planets Around the Sun*. New York: Scholastic Inc., 2002. A wonderful beginning reader on the Solar System with actual photographs of the sun, planets, and asteroids. Perfect for the primary class.

Note: Seymour Simon has written many books on the solar system, the stars and individual planets. Look for his other titles to be used as references or for children to look at in the classroom.

Wolf, Aline D. *How Big Is The Milky Way?*. Hollidaysburg, PA: Parent Child Press Inc., 2001. This little book relates the size of the Milky Way to the golden bead material in the Montessori classroom.

The Earth

Cole, Joanna. *The Magic School Bus Inside the Earth*. New York: Scholastic Inc., 1987. A class trip through the center of the Earth introduces earth science to children. This story is a favorite with my older primary students.

Frasier, Debra. *On the Day You Were Born*. New York: Harcourt Brace Jovanovich, Publishers, 1991. The Earth celebrates the birth of a newborn baby by offering its natural gifts to the child.

Gibbons, Gail. *Planet Earth/ Inside Out*. New York: Mulberry Books, 1998. This book introduces the earth's composition as a planet by taking us inside the earth.

Glaser, Linda. *Our Big Home, An Earth Poem*. New York: Scholastic Inc., 2000. An earth poem celebrating what we share on Earth, our one home. The illustrations are beautiful with an abundance of detail.

Lauber, Patricia. *You're Aboard Spaceship Earth*. New York: Scholastic Inc., 1998. A Let's-Read-and-Find-Out-Science book that explains how Planet Earth supports life and why it truly is Spaceship Earth.

Leutcher, Alfred. *Earth; Water;* Lloyd, David. *Air;* Satchwell, John. *Fire*. New York, NY: Pied Piper Book, 1984. Series of books on fire, Earth, air and water to help children understand each of the four elements. The text is longer, but still readable to children. (Three authors wrote this series)

McNulty, Faith. *How to Dig a Hole to the Other Side of the World*. New York: Scholastic Inc., 1990. The story takes us on an imaginary journey through the earth. It is a favorite with the older primary students.

Rockwell, Anne. *Our Earth*. New York: Scholastic Inc., 2000. In simple text and clear illustrations Anne explains our earth, it's characteristics, history and ecosystems.

Simon, Seymour, Nicole Fauteux. *Let's Try It Out in the Air* (Hands-On Early Learning Science Activities). New York: Scholastic Inc., 2002. This book, meant to be read to children, describes simple experiments And activities to observe the presence of air and its effects on things.

Singer, Marilyn. *On The Same Day in March, A Tour of The World's Weather*. New York: HarperCollins, 2000. This book takes us on a trip around the world exploring different areas on the same day. The pictures give children an awareness of the diversity on Earth in one moment of time.

Soutter-Perrot, Andrienne. *Air, Water, Fire and Earth. (A series of four books)* Mankato, MN: Creative Editions, 1993. Excellent series that is beautifully illustrated about the four elements of the Earth. Simple clear text.

Wolf, Aline D. *I Travel on Planet Earth.* Hollidaysburg, PA, Parent Child Press Inc., 2001. This little book explains the three different ways the earth is moving all at the same time.

Zolotow, Charlotte. *When The Wind Stops*. New York: Harper Collins, 1995. Charlotte Zolotow explains the cycles of day and night and the seasons, through a child's questions to his mom.

The Moon

Branley, Franklyn M.. *The Moon Seems to Change*. New York: HarperCollins, 1987. Let's read and find out series. Explains the phases of the moon. Branley has also written the book *What the Moon is Like*.

Bruchac, Joseph and Jonathan London. *Thirteen Moons on Turtle's Back, A Native American Year of Moons*. New York: Philomel Books, 1992. In poetry and paintings this book celebrates a Native American year through the full moons.

Carle. Eric. *Papa, please get the moon for me*. New York: Scholastic Inc., 1990. A little girl wants the moon and her Dad gets it for her. In the artwork we watch the phases of the moon.

Gibbons, Gail. *The Moon Book*. New York: Scholastic Inc., 1997. The clear illustrations and text describe the moon, its phases, eclipses, effects on the earth, and history. It also shares stories and legends about the moon.

Hamerstrom, Frances. *Walk When the Moon is Full*. Santa Cruz, CA: The Crossing Press, 1985. A family takes a walk each month when the moon is full and discovers the wonders of nature at night. Small chapter book to read to children.

Polacco, Patricia. *Meteor!*. New York: The Trumpet Club, 1993. Patricia tells us the story of a meteor, which landed in her grandparent's town when, as a child, she was visiting them for the summer.

Wheat, Janis Knudson. *Let's Go to the Moon*. Washington, D.C.: National Geographic Society, 1977. Photographs are used to illustrate this story of the Apollo 17 Flight to the moon and back to earth.

Wolf, Aline D. *I Know What Gravity Does*. Hollidaysburg, PA: Parent Child Press Inc., 2000. This little book shows how everything is held on the Earth by gravity.

Zolotow, Charlotte. *The Moon Was the Best*. New York: Greenwillow Books, 1993. A mother describes her visit to Paris to her daughter and shares her best memories.

Space Vehicles, Space Travel

Branley, Franklyn M. *The International Space Station*. New York: HarperCollins, 2000. This book explains the construction and purpose of the International Space Station and the life of the astronauts on board. The International Space Station is a collaborative project of many nations.

Becklake, Sue. *Traveling in Space*. Mahwah, New Jersey: Troll Associates, 1991. Interesting information on what happens inside a space station – just enough information for children to understand.

Butterfield, Moira. *Look Inside - Cross-Sections, Space.* New York: Dorling Kindersley Publishing Inc., 1994. A great book for children to explore when building their own spacecraft.

Keats, Ezra Jack. *Regards to the Man in the Moon*. New York: The Trumpet Club, 1991. This book is a story of a child and his parents who build a spaceship from "junk" that is fueled by imagination. If you build a cardboard spaceship, this is a fun story to share with the children.

Kerrod, Robin. *SPACECRAFT*. New York: Random House, 1989. Clear illustrations and short descriptions make this book easy to share with children.

Rockwell, Anne and David Brion. *Space Vehicles*. New York: Dutton Children's Books, 1994. This is an excellent introduction to space vehicles and their different functions.

Spizzirri, Peter M., Linda Spizzirri (editor). *An Educational Coloring Book of Space Craft*. Rapid City SD: Spizzirri Publishing Co. Inc., 1986.

_____. *An Educational Coloring Book of Shuttle Craft*. Spizzirri Publishing Co., Inc, 1986.

Both books have excellent black line drawings and clear descriptions and information on the different types of spacecraft. A perfect resource for children to create their own space vehicles.

Astronauts

Alston, Edith. *Let's Visit A Space Camp*. Mahwah, NJ: Troll Associates, 1990. This is a factual book about the NASA Space Camp at The Space and Rocket Center in Huntsville, Alabama. With photographs to support the text it shows how an astronaut is trained for outer space travel with simulators to replicate weightlessness. It also shows what attendees experience at Space Camp

Barton, Byron. *I Want To Be An Astronaut*. New York: Scholastic Inc., 1989. Simple clear text and illustrations of the jobs astronauts do in space. A classic book to read with children.

Lord, Suzanne and Jolie Epstein. *A Day in Space*. New York: Scholastic Inc., 1986. Using NASA photographs taken on a space shuttle mission, the authors describe what it is like to live and work in space. Easy to read to children.

Moche, Dinah L. *If You Were An Astronaut*. New York: A Golden Book, 1985. The photographs and text show what it would be like to be an astronaut spending a day in space.

Mullane, R. Mike. *Liftoff!* An Astronaut's Dream. Parsippany, N.J.: Silver Burdett Press, 1995. A chapter book describing Mike's personal experience as a mission specialist on the space shuttle. A read aloud for extended day.

Tan, Sheri. *Handshake in Space :The Apollo-Soyuz Test Project*. Norwalk, CT: Trudy Corporation, 1998. This is a Smithsonian Institute Odyssey book. Two children on a school field trip to the Smithsonian National Air and Space Museum imagine they are the U.S. and Russian astronauts and reenact the first rendezvous in space.

What Else is Out There?

Branley, Franklyn M. *Is There Life in Outer Space?* New York: HarperCollins, 1999. Discusses some of the ideas and mis-conceptions about life in outer space and speculates on the existence of such life in light of recent space explo-rations. A good read to begin to answer a child's question, "Is there any other life in space?"

Chaplin, Rob. *Alien Alphabet*. San Francisco: Chronicle Books, 1994. A fun flip book for students as they enjoy creating their own aliens by mixing and matching the pages.

Stewardship of the Earth

Asch, Frank. *The Earth and I*. San Diego: A Gulliver Green Book, Harcourt Brace Jovanovich, 1994. A child explains how she and the Earth are friends. The artwork is beautiful.

_____ *Water.* New York: Scholastic Inc., 1995. This book introduces different forms of water in simple text and colorful illustrations.

Benson, Laura Lee. *This is Our Earth.* Watertown, MA: Charlesbridge Publishing, 1994. A beautifully illustrated book shows the diversity of our Earth's inhabitants and creatures. The words can be sung and the song is included.

Cooney, Barbara. *Miss Rumphius.* New York: Puffin Books, 1982. This is a lovely story to show children how they can make a difference in their world by making it more beautiful.

Ehlert, Lois. *In My World.* New York: Harcourt Inc., 2002. The die cut pictures of objects in our natural world remind us of all we should be thankful for.

Jeffers, Susan. *Brother Eagle, Sister Sky.* New York: Dial Books, 1991. Susan Jeffers has illustrated Chief Seattle's message about respecting the Earth and taking care of it for future generations.

Lehrman, Fredric. *Loving the Earth, A Sacred Landscape Book for Children.* Berkeley, CA: Celestial Arts, 1990. This book explains the special features of our Earth and the need to take care of it.

Lindbergh, Reeve. *The Circle of Days.* New York: Scholastic Inc., 2000. The text is from the *Canticle of the Sun* by Saint Francis of Assisi.

Morrison, Meighan. *Long Live The Earth.* New York: Scholastic Inc., 1994. Patchwork quilt squares for illustrations and verse are used to remind us to take care of planet Earth.

Schimmel, Schim. *The Family of Earth.* New York: Scholastic Inc., 2002. This is a celebration in art and words of how, "The world may look different to each of us, but we all share the same earth."

_____.*Dear Children of the Earth, A Letter From Home.* Minnetonka, MN: Northwood Press, 1994. The Earth reminds us to take care of her and protect her for everyone's sake.

_____.*Children of the Earth...Remember.* 1997. The third in this series of books.

Thiele, Bob and George David Weiss. *What a Wonderful World.* New York: Scholastic Inc., 2000. Ashley Bryan illustrates with style the upbeat lyrics to this song.

Wolf, Aline D. *Pledge to the Earth.* Hollidaysburg, PA: Parent Child Press Inc., 2001. A daily pledge to remind children to do their part to respect and honor the Earth and its creatures.

My Place in Space

Banyai, Istvan. *Zoom.* New York: Viking, 1995. This book starts with a portion of a picture and continually steps us back to see more of it from a more distant perspective. It's not always what you expect to be next.

Cherry, Lynne. *The Armadillo From Amarillo.* San Diego, CA: A Gulliver Green Book, Harcourt Brace and Company, 1994. With the help of an eagle an armadillo gets to see his world beyond Texas.

Cuyler, Margery. *From Here to There.* New York: Scholastic, Inc. 2000. This book is a good read for the activity "My Place in Space," as a little girl discovers her place in the Universe.

Hartman, Gail. *As The Crow Flies.* (A first book of maps). New York: Aladdin Books (Macmillan Publishing Co.), 1993. A look at the world from the perspectives of an eagle, rabbit, crow, horse and gull. We become aware of the different maps of each of their worlds.

Hirst, Robin and Sally. *My Place in Space.* New York: Orchard Books, 1988. A child answers a bus driver's question. "Do you know where you live?." The answer is "yes out to the Universe." This book takes place in Australia and would be fun to compare with the children to a book answering the question from the North American perspective.

Nunn, Tamara, *My Global Address.* Cypress, A: Creative Teaching Press Inc., 1996. Simple text allows the child to read it alone.

Ross, Don and Sue Levytsky. *Where in The World is Walter? (A Book of Discovery).* Stamford, CT: Longmeadow Press, 1989. A fanciful perspective when a dog asks its mother, "Where am I? and she explains all the places he is in the Universe.

Sis, Peter. *Madlenka.* New York: Scholastic Inc, 2000. A little girl loses her tooth and walks around her block telling everyone she knows. A trip around her block is like a trip around the world.

Sweeney, Joan. *Me and My Place in Space.* New York: Scholastic Inc., 1999. An excellent read aloud to understand all the places we are at one time.

Wolf, Aline D. *I Live in the Universe.* Hollidaysburg, PA: Parent Child Press Inc., 2000. This simple book explains how a child lives in many places at the same time, ranging from a house to the universe.

Global Connections

Barner, Bob. *To Everything, There is a Season.* San Francisco, CA: Chronicle Books, 1998. This is a version of a verse from Ecclesiastes, which states there is a time for everything— even birth and death. Colorful, bold illustrations enhance the text.

Charlesworth, Liza. *Hats Around the World.* New York: Scholastic Inc., 1997. The photographs show people wearing different hats from around the world. The simple text is designed for a beginning reader. Each country of origin is noted!

G.T. Cunningham Elementary School. *We Are All Related, A Celebration of Our Cultural Heritage.* Vancouver, BC Canada: George T. Cunningham Elementary School, 1996. A celebration of cultural heritage expressed by children in their own words and in their own art.

Dr. Seuss, *The Butter Battle Book.* New York: Random House Inc., 1984. A humorous book in rhyme with an important message about conflict resolution.

Fox, Mem. *Whoever You Are.* New York: Harcourt Brace and Company, 1997. No matter how culturally different we may be, we are all the same inside. This is a beautiful book that celebrates diversity and is requested over and over in my class.

Gray, Nigel. *A Country Far Away.* New York: Orchard Books, 1988. This story parallels a child's day in Africa with the same day in the United States and shows how they accomplish the same tasks in each country.

Kabattchenko, M., V.. Kochurov, L. Kohanova, E. Kononenko, D. Kuznetsov, A. Lapitsky, V. Monakov, L. Stoupin and A. Zagonsky. *Peace in 100 Languages.* Rolling Hills Estate, CA: Jalmar Press, 1992. A one-word multilingual dictionary shows the word peace written in many languages. A great visual for the diversity of written languages. Also has famous quotes concerning peace.

LeTord, Bijou. *Peace on Earth, A Book of Prayer From Around the World.* New York: A Doubleday Book for Young Readers, 1992. This book has beautiful illustrations to accompany the poems. Each of the section pages is written in five languages.

Ommer, Vwe. *1000 Families*. Köln: Taschen, 2000. Beautiful photographs of families around the world. Descriptions in both German and English. A great book for children to look through. Book was published for UNICEF.

Rodgers, Fred. *The Giving Box*. Philadelphia, PA: Running Press Book Publishers, 2000. The book uses traditional stories and fables from around the world to illustrate the meaning of giving to others. The book comes with a little metal coin bank called The Giving Box to begin a tradition of giving with your children.

Scholes, Katherine. *Peace Begins with You*. San Francisco: Sierra Club Books/Little Brown and Company, 1989. With good suggestions for being peacemakers, this book shows how to talk about peace from personal and global perspectives.

Smith, David T. *If The World Were a Village*. Tonawanda, NY: Kids Can Press, Ltd., 2002. If the world were a village of 100 what would be the most prominent nationalities, languages, and resources available? Researched to reflect the population and resources of our larger world!

Thomas, Shelley Moore. *Somewhere Today, a Book of Peace*. Morton Grove, IL: Albert Whitman and Co., 1998. This book gives examples of how people can bring about peace by caring and helping each other. Good diversity in the photographs.

Wolf, Aline D. *I Offer You Peace*. Hollidaysburg, PA: Parent Child Press, 2000. A recitation based on the work of a nephew of Mohandas K. Gandhi.

Wood, Douglas. *Old Turtle*. Duluth, MN: Pfeifer-Hamilton Publishers, 1992. A fable that promotes a deeper understanding of the earth and our relationship with all its beings.

Reference Books for Children

Beginners World Atlas. National Geographic Society, Washington, DC: 1999. This is an excellent first atlas for a primary class. The maps of the continents are simple and clear with well-chosen photographs for each continent.

Collard, Sneed B. *Our Natural Homes*. Watertown, MA: Charlesbridge Publishing, 1996. Describes the various Earth ecosystems–tundra, mountains, deserts, forests, etc. It shows the diversity of regions on Earth.

Denne, Ben and Eileen O'Brien. *Usborne Discovery Internet-Linked Space*. New York: Scholastic Inc., 2002.*

Dowswell, Paul. *The Usborne First Encyclopedia of Space*. New York: Scholastic Inc., 2002. This book has wonderful visuals of images in space and explains many questions young children have in easy to understand text. It also includes over 40 Web sites for more information and pictures.

Howell, Laura, Kirsten Rogers and Corinne Henderson. *The Usborne Internet-Linked Library of Science, Earth, and Space*. New York: Scholastic Inc., 2002.*

Kindersley, Barnabas and Anabel. *Children Just Like Me*. New York: Dorling Kindersley Publishing Inc., Wonderful photographs of children from around the world sharing what they like to do. Written in association with UNICEF, it is excellent for understanding the diversity of cultures.

Taylor, Barbara. *The Animal Atlas (A Pictorial Atlas of World Wildlife)*. New York: Alfred A. Knopf, 1992. This is a great reference for animal habitats on every continent. Each region is highlighted within the continent itself and the animals of that region are identified and described..

*Usborne books have a series of Internet-Linked books that stand alone as a visual reference or you can visit the Web sites included to get more information on a particular topic. There are video clips and downloadable pictures that allow teachers to create materials for the classroom and enhance their lessons.

Van Rose, Susanna. *The Earth Atlas.* New York, NY: Dorling Kindersley Publishing Inc., 1994. This book explains the processes that made and shaped our Earth. Lots of visual images for children who ask a lot of questions.

Anthologies to Share with Children

Caduto, Michael J. and Joseph Bruchac. *Keepers of the Night.* Golden, CO: Falcrum Publishing, 1994. Native American Stories and Nocturnal Activities for Children.

Caduto, Michael J. *Earth Tales from Around the World.* Golden, CO: Fulcrum Publishing, 1997. Includes folktales from around the world with related lessons to do with children. The stories explore concepts of the Earth, sky, fire, water, seasons and weather, plants, animals, circle of life, stewardship and wisdom. A great resource for adding stories to content.

Milord, Susan. *Tales of the Shimmering Sky.* Charlotte, VT: Williamson Publishing, 1996. This book includes ten global folktales with activities related to the stories. It is beautifully illustrated.

Monroe, Jean Guard and Ray A. Williamson. *They Dance in the Sky, Native American Star Myths.* Boston: Houghton Mifflin Company, 1987. This is a collection of legends from various Native American cultures about the stars and constellations.

References Books for Teachers

A Klutz Guide. *Backyard Stars.* Palo Alto, CA: Klutz, 1998. A laminated folder with star charts for each season. They are for use with just your eyes, no binoculars needed. Also great for the Star Bag.

Carson, Rachel,. *The Sense of Wonder.* New York: HarperCollins Publishers, 1998. A must read for all adults who work with children.

Daleo, Morgan Simone. *Curriculum of Love.* Charlottesville, VA: Grace Publishing and Communications, 1996. This book shares activities to cultivate the spiritual nature of the child.

Duffy, Michael and D'Neil. *Children of the Universe, Cosmic Education in the Montessori Classroom.* Hollidaysburg, PA: Parent Child Press Inc., 2002. The first complete book on cosmic education for the elementary years.

Henbest, Nigel. *The Night Sky.* Usborne Spotter's Guides. New York: Scholastic Inc., 1996. Beside each object in the book is a circle for you to check off what you have seen. This is a practical way to keep a record of your observations.

Mechler, Gary. *The Night Sky.* National Audubon Society First Field Guide. New York: Scholastic Inc., 1999. A reference book with many details but still has the beginner in mind.

Pasachoff, Jay M. *Astronomy.* Peterson First Guides. Boston: Houghton Mifflin Company, 1988. A simplified field guide to the stars, planets, and the universe.

Pogue, William R. *How do you go to the Bathroom in Space?.* New York: A Tom Doherty Associate Book, 1991. This book is written in question and answer format. It will answer many questions children may have. It is also a valuable source of information for teachers.

Smith, Alastair and Corinne Henderson. *The Usborne Internet-Linked Library of Science Energy, Forces and Motion.* New York: Scholastic Inc., 2002. Great resource for physical science concepts, i.e. gravity.

Warren, Jean. *Great Big Themes Space.* Torrance, CA: Totline Publication, A Division of Frank Schaffer Publications Inc., 1991. A resource for activities to do with children. Especially good are the ABC's of space vocabulary cards!

Wolf, Aline D. *Our Peaceful Classroom.* Hollidaysburg, PA: Parent Child Press Inc., 1991. A narrative describing a Montessori classroom illustrated by students from Montessori Schools around the world. A delightful book to read to your class and to share with parents.

_____. *Nurturing the Spirit in non-sectarian classrooms.* Hollidaysburg, PA.: Parent Child Press Inc., 1996. This pivotal book for teachers focuses on Maria Montessori's greatest desire to create a better world by nurturing the spirit of each child.

_____. *Peaceful Children, Peaceful World.* Hollidaysburg, PA: Parent Child Press Inc., 1991. Using dramatic illustrations by Joe Servello, this book highlights Montessori's quotations on peace.

Other Titles Available from Parent Child Press

Children of the Universe, Cosmic Education in the Montessori Elementary Classroom
Nurturing the Spirit in Non-Sectarian Classroom
Peaceful Children, Peaceful World
Our Peaceful Classroom
Andy and His Daddy
Look at the Child
Cosmic Wonder Series
Thoughtful Living Series
Sense of Wonder Series
You Are an Artist
Child-Size Masterpieces Series for Art Appreciation

Parent Child Press Inc. • PO Box 675 • Hollidaysburg PA 16648

Toll Free 866-727-3682 • www.parentchildpress.com **• e-mail** pcp@nb.net

Address for Classroom Resources

The Astronomical Society of the Pacific
390 Ashton Avenue
San Francisco CA 94112
Phone (415) 337-1100 Fax (415) 337-1100
www.astrosociety.org./
Curriculum, catalog of items

Carolina Biological Supply Company
2700 York Road
Burlington NC 27215
Phone (800) 334-5551 Fax (800) 222-7112
carolina@carolina.com
www.carolina.com
Solar Oven, Basic Solar Kit
and many resources

For Spacious Skies
111 Brickyard Road
Athol MA –1331
jjborden@webtv.net
www.forspaciousskies.com
Curriculum, Cloud Chart and posters

in-print for children
12 E. Glenside Avenue
Glenside PA 19038
Phone (215) 885-2722 Fax (800) 481-1981
inprint@earthlink.net
www.in-printforchildren.com
Constellation cards and daytime/nighttime cards

How the Weatherworks
301 Creek Valley Lane
Rockville MD 20850
Phone (301) 990-9324 FAX (630) 563-1782
webmaster@weatherworks.com
www.weatherworks.com
Cloud 9 flash card sets

Michael Olaf
65 Ericson Court #1
Arcata CA 95521
Phone (888) 880-9235 Fax (800) 427-8877
michaelola@ao.com
www.michaelolaf.com
Star guides, books, prisms

Montessori Services
11 West Barham Avenue
Santa Rosa CA 95407
Phone (877-975-3003 or (707) 579-3003
Fax (800) 483-9822
info@montessoriservices.com
www.montessoriservices.com
Sundial, trays and containers

National Geographic Society
PO Box 98199
Washington DC 20090-8199
Phone (800) 647-5463 (general information)
askngs@nationalgeographic.com
www.nationalgeographic.com
Curriculum, books, globes (including inflatable
globe of the Earth) and other resources.

PaperCuts
1428 SE 4th Avenue Unit 1-267
Deerfield Beach FL 33441
Phone 800-995-0014 Fax 954-428-6893
Papermont@aol.com
Black Line Masters for Montessori Classroom
Materials

Parent Child Press Inc.
PO Box 675
Hollidaysburg PA 1 6648
Phone (866) 727-3686 or (814)696-7512
Fax (814) 696-7510
pcp@nb.net
www.parentchildpress.com
Subject appropriate books for teachers
and children.

Priority Montessori Materials
3920 P Road
Paonia CO 81428
Phone (970) 527-7588 Fax (970) 527-7590
pmmaterial@aol.com
Earth model for layers of the earth, moon phase,
Cards, Solar System Model and cards

Ranger Rick Magazine
National Wildlife Federation
11100 Wildlife Center Drive
Reston VA 20190-5362
Phone (703) 438-6000
Phone orders (717) 461-3092
www.nwf.org
Curriculum and resources

Scholastic Book Clubs Inc.
2931 E. McCarty St.
PO Box 7503
Jefferson City MO 65102-7503
Phone (800) 724-6527
Fax (800- 223-4011
www.scholastic.com/bookclubs
Books, Usborne internet-linked books
Night Sky Planetarium Kit

Spizzirri Publishing Company, Inc.
PO Box 9397
Rapid City SD 57709
Phone (800) 325-9819 Fax (800) 322-9819
spizzpub@aol.com
www.spizzirri.com
Books and educational coloring books

Totline Publications
PO Box 2250
Everett WA 98203
Curriculum on Space that includes
ABC's of Space Vocabulary cards.

Troll Book Clubs
4600 Pleasant Hill
Memphis TN 38118
Phone (888) 998-7655
troll@aegiscomgroup.com
www.troll.com
Rocket model, balloon rocket kit,
Books

Uncle Milton Industries
5717 Corsa Avenue
Westlake Village CA 91362
Phone (818) 707-0800
Fax (818) 707-0878
info@unclemilton.com
www.unclemilton.com
Star Theater, Star Theater 2

Waseca Learning Environments
580 Tallassee
Athens GA 30606
Phone (706) 546-8833 Fax (706) 613-0133
www.wasecalearning.com
Sun for birthday walk, world rug and
animal figures for different continents

Additional Websites to Visit

The Nine Planets
www.seds.org/nineplanets

NASA
www.spacelink.nasa.gov/products
lithographs, videos, posters, curriculum

Earth & Sky Report
www.earthsky.com/

Hubble Space Telescope
http://hubble.stsci.edu/

Sky & Telescope Magazine
www.skypub.com

Astronomy Magazine
www.astronomy.com

Glossary

Alien – 1. A person born in and owing allegiance to a country other than the one in which he lives.
   2. A nonterrestial being that can be imagined, but, as of yet, not proven to exist.

Asteroid – A celestial body, or very small planet, whose orbit lies chiefly between Mars and Jupiter; also called a planetoid.

Asteroid Belt – The many asteroids that are orbiting in the area between Mars and Jupiter.

Astronaut – A person trained in or engaged in space flight.

Atmosphere – The air that surrounds Planet Earth.

Axis – A real or imaginary straight line passing through an object and on which that object rotates. e.g. Earth rotates on its axis.

Chrysalis – The third stage in the life of the butterfly. When the caterpillar is mature, it develops a covering of hard, smooth skin and becomes a chrysalis from which the butterfly eventually emerges.

Comet – A luminous heavenly body, usually irregular in form, often having a long tail and following an orbit about the sun.

Constellation – Any of various configurations of stars to which names have been given.

Galaxy – A large system of stars held together by mutual gravitation and isolated from similar systems by vast regions of space.

Gravitation – The attraction that large masses of matter have for each other. The sun's gravitation holds the planets in their orbits. The moon's gravitation pulls at the oceans and causes the tides to rise and fall.

Gravity – The same as gravitation, but it particularly relates to the attraction of the earth for objects near its surface.

Luminous – Shining; emitting or reflecting light.

Meteor – A translucent fiery streak in the sky produced by a disintegrating meteoroid passing through the Earth's atmosphere.

Meteoroid – Any of the small bodies, usually remnants of comets, traveling through space.

Milky Way – The faintly luminous band stretching across the heavens, composed of innumerable stars too distant to be seen clearly with the naked eye; the galaxy containing the Earth, sun and solar system.

Nitrogen – A colorless, odorless gas that constitutes about four-fifths of the volume of the atmosphere. It is one of the substances necessary for life in plants and animals.

Observatory – A building with large telescopes for making detailed observations of the sky.

Orbit – The curved path, usually elliptical, on which a planet or satellite travels.

Orion – A constellation named for a giant-sized hunter in mythology.

Oxygen – A life-giving gas that is colorless and odorless, constituting about one fifth of the volume of the atmosphere. When anything burns, it unites with oxygen.

Planet – Any of the nine large heavenly bodies revolving about the sun and shining by reflected light.

Planetarium – 1. An apparatus or model representing the solar system. 2. A device for projecting celestial images on the inner surface of a dome. 3. A building containing such a device with seats for an audience.

Prism – A transparent solid object, used for dispersing light into a spectrum or for reflecting rays of light.

Satellite – A body that revolves around a planet, such as a moon. A man-made device launched from the Earth into orbit around a planet or the sun.

Spectrum – The band of colors produced when sunlight is passed through a prism.

About the Authors

Aline and Joanne combining their ideas for this book.

Joanne Alex has been honored many times as an outstanding teacher of young children. In addition to being named Teacher of the Year for the State of Maine in 1998, she received the 1994 National Outstanding Environmental Educator of the Year Award from the American Tree Foundation and the 1995 Maine Audubon Society's Teacher of the Year Award. Joanne was selected in 1993 to attend the National Geographic Summer Geography Institute and in 1999 the National Geographic Society Alliance Leadership Academy. In 1996 she received an award from the Maine Association for Quality Child-Care and most recently she was named a state finalist for the 2002 Presidential Award for Excellence in Science Education.

Joanne is a cum laude graduate of Colby College and received a Master of Education degree in Environmental Science Education from the University of Maine. After earning her diploma from the St. Nicholas Training Centre for the Montessori Method of Education, she was certified by the American Montessori Society. With her husband, Joe, she founded the Stillwater Montessori School in Old Town, Maine in 1983, where she is currently the head teacher and education director.

Joanne, Joe, and their three children have long been active in the Children's International Summer Village program where they interact every year with children from foreign countries.

Aline Wolf, author of 25 books, has long been regarded as a modern interpreter of Maria

Montessori's philosophy and methods. In 1961 with her husband, Gerald, she founded Penn-Mont Academy, the first Montessori school to be licensed in Pennsylvania and the third in the nation. Her best-known book, *A Parents' Guide to the Montessori Classroom*, is now a classic in the Montessori world and has been translated into Spanish, French and Chinese. In subsequent books, Aline highlighted Montessori's insights for parenting, and for teaching peace. She also developed an art appreciation program for young children featuring a manual and a series of art postcard books entitled *Child-Size Masterpieces*. With the publication of her pivotal book, *Nurturing the Spirit in Non-Sectarian Classrooms*, she narrowed her focus to the most important aspect of all Montessori's educational work—attaining peace by nurturing the spirit of the child, particularly in the framework of cosmic education. Her most recent publications are a series of Cosmic Wonder Books for children.

Aline holds a B.A. degree from Marywood University, a Montessori Diploma from The St. Nicholas Training Centre, London, and honorary degrees of Doctor of Pedagogy from St. Francis University, Loretto, PA, and from Marywood University, Scranton, PA.

Acknowledgements

I want to thank:

My parents, Vito and Frances DeFilipp and my brothers—Richard, Peter and Tim—for all their support, love and belief in my work;

My friend and walking partner, Karen Wihbey, who gave me moral support throughout this project;

The Stillwater Montessori School Community (staff, parents and students) for their help and patience throughout this project;

Aline Wolf, to whom this book owes its concept and completion, and whose encouragement and help goes beyond any words I can find;

Peggy Curran, who typed several versions of this manuscript and whose suggestions and expertise greatly enhanced its quality;

Catherine Maresca, Jessica Alex, Ming Tang, Paul Conway, Mary Truesdale, Cheryl Colley, Gerald Wolf, Frank Wihbey and Mary Zajac, who read the manuscript and offered helpful suggestions;

My husband, Joe Alex, whose loving support for many years has made possible all my experience in the classroom and who eased my burden of this undertaking with his daily encouragement and technical assistance;

And finally, I want to acknowledge my original inspiration for this work—Maria Montessori and her vision of peaceful children bringing about a peaceful world.

J. D. A.